In the Blink
of an Eye

ALI BACON

¶

Published by Linen Press, London 2018
8 Maltings Lodge
Corney Reach Way
London
W4 2TT
www.linen-press.com

A CIP catalogue record for this book is available from the British Library.

Front cover photograph: Charlotte Hill, 1839–1862. Daughter of David
Octavius Hill, David Octavius Hill and Robert Adamson
© National Galleries of Scotland
Flowers design: Olga_Spb / Freepik
Back cover photograph: Calton Hill, Edinburgh c1870,
unknown photographer, by permission Rob Douglas,
http://www.papershadowsandlight.com/
Cover design: Zebedee Design, Edinburgh
Typeset in Sabon by Zebedee Design, Edinburgh
Printed and bound by Lightning Source

ISBN 9780993599729

About the Author

After graduating from St Andrews University, Ali Bacon worked in Oxford's Bodleian Library where she found a cache of famous Victorian photographs, sparking a life-long interest in early photographers. *In the Blink of an Eye* follows her first novel, *A Kettle of Fish* (Thornberry 2012) and marries her passion for fiction and photography. Chapters from *In the Blink of an Eye* have already been successful in local and national short story competitions. Ali lives near Bristol where she is active in the local writing community.

Dedicated to

The St Andrews Photography Festival

2016–

People in this Book

In St Andrews

Sir David Brewster (1781-1868), *scientist and inventor,
Principal of St Andrews University*

Dr John Adamson (1809-1870), *physician and university
lecturer, second son of the Adamson family of Burnside
Farm*

Jane Adamson (1813-c1860), *John's younger sister*

Robert Adamson (1821-1848), *John's younger brother,
moved to Edinburgh in 1843*

In Edinburgh

Walter Fairlie (1797-1856), *minister of the Free Church
of Scotland in Gilmerton*

David Octavius (D.O.) Hill (1802-1870), *artist and
Secretary to the Royal Scottish Academy*

Charlotte Hill, later Charlotte Dalgleish, (1839-1862),
D.O.'s daughter

Jessie Mann (1805-1867), *a family friend of D.O. Hill*

Amelia Paton, later Amelia Hill (1821-1904), *from
Dunfermline in Fife, sister of the artist* Joseph Noel
Paton

Elizabeth Rigby, later Lady Eastlake, (1809-1893), *English art critic living in Edinburgh, moved to London in 1849*

Margaret Kemp (1808-1889), *wife of George Meikle Kemp, architect of Edinburgh's Scott Monument*

Elizabeth Hall (dates unknown), *a fishwife in the village of Newhaven*

Mary Brodie (1842-1911), *daughter of sculptor,* William Brodie, *married to* James Gowans, *architect*

Author's note: *Malcolm Scobie,* minister of the Free Church of Scotland in Blairgowrie and *Giacomo Buonarotti,* assistant administrator of the Academia di Arte in Carrara, are entirely fictional.

Acknowledgements

My biggest debt is to previous writers on Hill and Adamson who provided me with both inspiration and a springboard of historical fact. Please refer to the list of Selected Books, Articles and Web Resources for details.

Many others helped with research along the way: Anne Cruikshank provided notes on an ancestor who was a member of the Great Disruption (and I hope she doesn't mind that I added a few years to his life); novelist Catherine Czerkawska sent generous information on the area around Mauchline in Ayrshire and Rob Douglas of www.papershadowsandlight.com provided much-needed help with details of the calotype process.

The result of this project is a relatively short book but at times it felt like a mammoth task. Huge thanks go to Gail, Jean, Jane, Jo, Nicola and other members of Bristol Women Writers who saw the idea from its infancy through a long and troubled adolescence. Writer John Holland also helped massively by championing me and Silver Harvest at Stroud Short Stories and beyond. Thanks also to Bobbie, Penny and Dorothy who read the 7000 words which grew into the final book, to Penny again for accompanying me on expeditions to museums and graveyards around the country and to Geoff for not minding my corresponding absences. My brother-in-law George deserves a mention too for hoarding his old copies of The Scots Magazine and finding them when required. Lynn Michell of Linen Press made my happiness complete by liking the book just as it was. Huge appreciation goes to her for her support and patient editing.

My final thanks are to Rachel Nordstrom of St Andrews University Special Collections whose invitation to the St

Andrews Photography Festival introduced me to a whole community of early photography enthusiasts. Because I hope it will bring their heroes more of the fame they deserve, this book is dedicated to them.

CONTENTS

AN ENDING

CHAPTER ONE

The Hour and the Day

May 1866

Before he left for Edinburgh, Malcolm Scobie, minister of the Free Kirk in Blairgowrie, spoke to his housekeeper and to his beadle, explaining he'd be gone for two days but back in plenty of time to compose his Sunday sermon. He also took it into his head to write to Louisa.

My Dear,

I am on my way to Auld Reekie for the first time in all these years, and I can't bring the place to mind without thinking of you. The pretext for my journey is the unveiling of the Disruption Painting, and in seeing it I plan to celebrate the very thing it depicts – the day in '43 when four hundred ministers, my good self amongst them, walked away from a church beholden to earthly masters and set up a Free Kirk which truly glorifies God.

Of course, my dearie, I know only too well how, on that day, I threw away both your father's trust and your affection. Nor have I told you how much it vexed me, and so I am telling you now, albeit belatedly, of the doubts that assailed me then and still, in the wee small hours, wing their way into my thoughts and perturb my dreams.

You will remember, I'm sure, how every dissenting minister was photographed by the artist, Mr D.O. Hill, captured in the blink of an eye, so that he could include us in the painting at his leisure. When I see myself in that company and am reminded of my part in God's work, surely I will cast my doubts aside.

Your father was right to warn me that my existence after the Disruption would be a mean and difficult one and I never did blame you for not following me on my Great Adventure. In all that time of missing you, I prayed you found warmth and companionship with your family or, even better, the love of a less troubled and troublesome soul than mine.

If this letter reaches you (I am sending it to your father's house) you may like to think of me embarking on this shorter journey in which I mark the ending of the one I began so long ago.

May God's Blessings be on you!
Your loving friend,
Malcolm Scobie

He sealed the letter and addressed it. He might as well post it in Edinburgh and so he laid it between the pages of the Bible he would carry with him on his way.

After spending the night with an uncle in Granton, Scobie took an omnibus to Princes Street and walked eastwards to the Calton Rooms where the painting was on display. The Monument to Scott, completed not long after the Disruption, soared upwards but he did not let his eyes follow its spire into the heavens or allow his thoughts to linger on the marble figures gazing down on him from their lofty plinths. There would be time to wonder at man's ingenuity when he had made his peace with God.

At the junction of the North Bridge, where all of Edinburgh converged in a hubbub, he was obliged to stop. Carriages clattered up from Leith Row, wheeling into the station where he had disembarked the night before, or carried on up the cobbles to the Old Town. Folk going about their business pushed past those who had come only to stop and stare. Above them, sea-gulls wheeled and dipped towards a group of fishwives standing with their creels on the corner, their cries of *Caller herring!* as piercing as those of the birds. The whiff of sea air was something he had missed in Perthshire.

In the Calton Convening Rooms, those whom God or Art had brought together were enjoying a morning of conviviality. If Scobie had come in search of reverential silence, he had come at the wrong time. Under the lantern ceiling, the noise of conversation, in some cases disputation, rose around and above him like a cloud of bees let out from a hive. The painting – so big it spanned the whole room – was on a dais raised above the floor by a good four feet, but Scobie was too far from it to get a feel for any of the detail or to distinguish where the human flesh of the onlookers ended and the oil paint began. It was at least to his advantage that he was neither especially tall nor encumbered by a companion and he was able, by squirming between tailcoats and sidestepping out-thrust elbows, to manoeuvre his way to the very front row of onlookers and take in the painted scene that was the cause of such excitement.

Scobie had never had the opportunity to appreciate art other than the stained glass windows in the kirk of his childhood and the engraved plates in books kept at home on a shelf he couldn't reach until he was ten. In fact his interest in Louisa had been piqued by her resemblance to a plate in one of those books which had the name *Gainsborough* printed underneath.

Neither this nor anything else had prepared him for what he now saw. The ministers were painted, row upon row, in a manner that made each countenance lifelike. Their bodies were by comparison strangely uniform, and as a result each face bore an individuality that verged on the grotesque. Unnerved by so many eyes looking back at him, Scobie instinctively stepped back.

A voice at his elbow said, 'What do you think?'

Another man of the cloth had joined him. His grey grizzled hair and deeply furrowed forehead put him twenty years older than Scobie.

'I've never seen anything like it,' Scobie said.

The stranger stretched out a hand. 'Walter Fairlie, Gilmerton.'

Scobie returned the handshake. 'Malcolm Scobie, from Blairgowrie.'

Fairlie was frowning at the painting, his eyes moving slowly from face to face while Scobie studied the overall composition. In the centre of the painting, Thomas Chalmers, leader of the Disruption, stood in a pool of light, as if receiving the blessing of Heaven. In front of him the leaders of the new Kirk were signing the Deed of Demission, the pledge that would free them from their old dispensations. Around this group, the dissenting ministers, riding a swell of emotion, made a sea of bobbing heads.

'He has Chalmers, that's for sure,' Scobie said.

Fairlie had lapsed into silence which he broke by throwing back his head and giving a bark of laughter. Scobie followed the line of his finger and had no trouble recognising his companion in the painting, just to the left of centre. Twenty years might have passed but not much had changed in the face of Walter Fairlie, except that it was now wreathed in smiles.

'That's you all right,' Scobie said.

Try though he might, he found it hard to pick himself out, perhaps because filling the background and the corners, and insinuating themselves into the crowd of ministers, were faces belonging to all manner of folk, few of whom he recognised.

Walter Fairlie was clearly better versed in Edinburgh society and jogged his memory. 'Hugh Miller,' he said of a tartan-clad figure in the foreground. Miller, a writer and Chalmers' staunch ally had died, Scobie thought, some time ago. The same could likely be said of many others. From that day to this was a span of twenty-three years.

Just off centre there was a striking figure with dark blond hair – Mr Hill, the artist. Behind him stood a young man, ignoring the crowd as he peered downwards into a box, a camera in fact. Scobie groped for his name. 'Hill's partner? He was never there that day.'

Fairlie nodded. 'Robert Adamson, I remember, from St Andrews.' He grimaced, and laid his finger by his nose. 'Artistic license, isn't that what they cry it?'

Scobie puffed out his cheeks. If the painting celebrated churchmen, it was others that caught the eye: a group of fishermen peeking in at the skylight, on one side a crowd of women in the fashions of the day, and, in the foreground, a man in Eastern dress.

'So what about you?' Fairlie said.

Edging closer to the front, Scobie scanned the faces again. He tried to remember were he had stood and who had been next to him, but that was no help. The artist had repositioned everything and everybody. A few friends and teachers from his student days slid into familiar focus but most remained stubbornly unknown.

The air in the room was dense with the heat of the crowd and beside him Fairlie shifted in discomfort. Scobie stepped back and said, 'Let's go.' One thing was clear. Half the folk of Edinburgh might be in the painting, but he was not among them.

Outside on the pavement, the two men drew breath.

'Did you no sit for a calotype?' Fairlie said.

Straight ahead, only a few hundred yards away, was a row of grey stone houses set on the flank of Calton Hill. Had Scobie imagined entering a dim parlour in the furthest of them, waiting his turn for the camera? He shrugged away his confusion. 'I mind it well. Two days after the Disruption, I was called to Rock House. My picture was taken outside, with three others.'

These days the camera was commonplace. Mrs Dewar, the

organist's wife, had recently got herself *cartes de visites*, the cause of some rolling of eyes. *Who will she call on who doesn't already ken her?* they said. Nor was the photograph a thing of great beauty, although its subject had by all accounts bought a new hat for the occasion. He did not think that Louisa, who had stopped answering his letters after a month, would have a *carte de visite*, though if she had a husband, they might have a family picture on the sideboard.

Back in '43, calotypes, as they called them, had been entirely new. As Scobie sat in line, a Bible on his knees, he had thought of how God would surely reward him for his faith. In that moment he'd been blind to the sacrifices ahead: or maybe as guilty of hubris as any of those who had cleaved to the old Kirk.

'The sun was in our eyes. I mind that,' Fairlie joined in with his own reminiscence, 'but yon Hill kept our spirits up, chaffing us about being bathed in the Light of Righteousness.'

Scobie's laugh was without humour. 'Or the limelight. Whichever it was, it did me no favour, since he didn't think to put me in the picture.'

Fairlie gave him a sideways look. 'Or in the years that have passed, maybe some of they calotypes just got lost.'

Quite likely, thought Scobie, but it was hard not to find some irony in his absence from the painting he had come all this way to see. Could it even be some comment on his own plight – a soul that had got lost along with the artist's photograph?

He shook himself, as if something hidden in the folds of his cassock might fall out and reveal itself; his younger self, the purpose of his visit. Nor was it just the absence of his face that rankled. 'I never had much understanding of the arts.'

'You don't like it then, the painting?'

Scobie sighed. 'I'd just like to know how he set about it and what meaning there is to all those folk being there.'

'I daresay he had his reasons,' Fairlie said, 'artistic or

otherwise.' He was looking up and down the street which was as hectic as when Scobie had arrived. 'So will I see you at the Assembly?'

The showing of the painting had been planned to coincide with the annual meeting of the Free Kirk. Scobie shook his head. 'I've never been a delegate. And I need to be away home.' He had hoped to go back to Blairgowrie with new conviction and a glowing report of the painting. The kirk session might even order a copy and the congregation admire his place in it. Now the only topic he could think of for his Sunday sermon was vanity and how he had fallen prey to its temptations.

'If you came only for the painting,' Fairlie said. 'I'm no surprised you're disappointed.' He looked at Scobie directly, his eyes as sharp as flints. With a jolt of awareness, Scobie felt called to account. 'But if you have an hour to spare, why don't we go back there, you and I?'

Back where? Scobie might have asked, but Fairlie was already on his way, not along Princes Street or following the pavement that turned towards Waverly Bridge, but across the busy road. Scobie could do nothing but wait for a gap in the welter of traffic and follow in his wake.

And so they stood, as they had done all those years before, in front of St Andrews Kirk, the tallest and most graceful spire in the city. Fairlie's eyes were on the spot where the steeple disappeared into the milky haze of the mid-day sky.

'Come, and the works that God hath wrought with admiration see.'

The psalmist's response came easily to Scobie,

'In his working to the sons of men, most terrible is He.'

Fairlie's grunt was dismissive. 'St Andrews was always a wee bit fancy for the Dissenters.'

Scobie knew from bitter experience that a ramshackle church was no encouragement to worship but he laughed his agreement. He felt the buds of a new friendship forming and would not

21

be the one to stunt their growth. Opening his shoulders to the air blowing up from the Forth, he felt an awakening that hadn't taken place in front of the painting. Maybe the day wasn't wasted after all.

Fairlie must have caught the change in his mood. 'A painting is just a painting and will be more pleasing to some than to others. What matters is the part we play.' Again the flinty look. 'So will we go?'

This time there was no doubting his meaning. They would walk from the spot where they had left the old Assembly and retrace the steps the dissenters had taken: up and over Hanover Street, Dundas Street and Pitt Street; by Brandon Street and Canon Mills, over the Water of Leith to Tanfield Hall, the incongruous building where the new Kirk had been born.

They kept to an even pace as far as the crowded pavements allowed.

'You must have been new to the ministry back then,' Fairlie said.

'I was only just ordained.'

And full of the neophyte's fervour, the desire for faith, for absolute conviction. The Kirk needed to be freed from the shackles of the landowners and the courts. It was the cost that still rankled.

'I was sent to a country parish.' His first living, if you could call it that, had tested him with its devout but poor congregation. There were hardly enough of them to support a minister.

'We must go where we are called,' Fairlie said.

Which is what he had told Louisa. 'Why don't you just stop up your ears?' she had said. 'Can you not serve God and be paid for it?' She didn't understand that in the old Kirk there was no security, not any longer.

Where the pavement narrowed, he and Fairlie stopped to let a heavy carriage trundle past. 'And have you always been in Gilmerton?' Scobie knew of the village, just west of the city.

'We were lucky. My wife and I had means and we bought

our own house. The congregation pulled together and built a new Kirk close by, not the most handsome, but you know what the Lord said. *Where two or three are gathered together.*'

The text was all too familiar. In Scobie's first tenure, they struggled to find anywhere to worship. As for living quarters, he had a box-bed in the home of one of the elders whose wife's staple offering of boiled neeps never left the fabric of the building. It was five years before he was called to the town of Blairgowrie, with its new manse and more appreciative flock.

'There's a Mrs Scobie?'

He shook his head. 'There was somebody, here in Edinburgh, but her father was against it.'

'Och, that's lang syne,' Fairlie objected. 'The job's far easier with a lady in the manse.'

Scobie was impressed by Fairlie's understanding. The ministry might be a vocation but the carrying out of it was a job, one that was made easier by having a companion. Amongst his congregation there were two sisters who invited him to their home on a regular basis and plied him with as many drams or cups of tea as the season allowed. Elspeth Crawford, daughter of the session clerk and a teacher in the Sunday School, was kind to him in ways a man who cultivated loneliness didn't deserve. But he had brushed Elspeth aside, knowing that in his heart he only had room for Louisa. He felt in his pocket for his Bible and the letter folded inside.

On the brow of the hill they stopped to get their breath back. Tanfield was hidden by the fall in the land yet the Forth, with its fishing boats and morning haars, looked only a step away. Scobie examined the buildings on either side of the street, looking for the faces that had crammed the windows as the ministers filed past. They stared back at him, empty, except for one where the curtain was drawn aside only to be quickly pulled back again. One thing could never be regained: the silence of the solemn procession of '43 was obliterated here, as everywhere else, by the clatter of wheels and the rumble of distant trains.

The Moorish roof of Tanfield rose into view. The old gasworks hall was an odd place for the ministers to meet but the only room close enough and big enough to hold them all. As he and Fairlie crossed over the Water of Leith, bloated with spring rain, the silent shadow of the hall loomed over them and Scobie's heart became a weight in his chest. 'Will we go in?'

He stepped forward to try the door but it was locked. Fairlie, closer to him than he realised, spoke in his ear and Scobie was shocked by the warmth of the old man's breath on his cheek. 'I maun leave you now. For I'm away home and only you can find what you came for.'

Scobie, expecting he and Fairlie would walk together back to Princes Street, was caught out. He would have offered thanks for the other man's company, but Fairlie was already walking away and didn't hear the farewell Scobie called after him.

The sun had dimmed to pewter. The pilgrimage was over and Scobie knew that neither his faith nor his belief in his Kirk would be rekindled by a closed door or an event he could barely remember.

He was struggling to bring to mind the scene in Tanfield that day, tease out his own recollection and take some guidance from it, but the scale and vividness of Hill's version, the force of what Fairlie had called its artistic licence, had swept away the reality. The swathe of Edinburgh society overshadowed the seriousness of the signing of the Deed. What Hill had created was not what Scobie had seen.

Scobie turned back to the city. Try as he might to dislodge it, Hill's picture stuck in his mind. His mother had always said that art was untrustworthy.

He felt the weariness of a long day and a fruitless journey. The question posed by Fairlie about why he had come to Edinburgh lurked under his skin like a skelf. The painting was a symbol of the Disruption and his part in it. His absence from it seemed to throw the same question back at him, not only why he had done as he did, but the meaning of all the years that had passed in between.

Only you can find what you came for.

Scobie trudged back up the hill, asking himself why the painting had taken on so much importance or whether the real reason for his journey was something else.

Throughout the day his hands had strayed to the letter in his pocket. He could have posted it in Blairgowrie or on Princes Street. He didn't need to take it out to read the address. He was no more than a mile from Louisa's father's house. Who was to say she might not still be there?

A man coming towards him saw his vestments and nodded a respectful greeting which Scobie returned. He straightened his shoulders. Many of those in the Disruption Painting were long gone. Malcolm Scobie was the minister of Blairgowrie Free Kirk and had more to offer than the newly ordained minister of '43.

Whatever had happened to Louisa, it was time to let her know.

EXPOSURE

CHAPTER TWO

Harebells in Barley

St Andrews, March 1843

Jane Adamson watched the rain come in from the sea, casting its veil over the fields and hedgerows around the farm. By noon there was a suspicion of blue in the mist, like harebells in barley. When she'd taken the washing down from the pulley, she went to find her mother and said, 'I'm away to St Andrews.' Her mother's silence required a response. 'I could do with stretching my legs.'

At the top of the hill, beyond the church, the rain stopped and she took the coast path, shaking off the air of the farm kitchen – a steamy blanket that could give warmth and comfort or cling like a hair shirt. The conversation at home never changed: the weather and the washing, the price of beef in Cupar. Up here she could watch the sea shift under the changing sky and the gulls swoop over the Spindle Rock, knowing she would soon round the headland to where the skyline was punctured by the rooftops and spires of St Andrews.

She dropped down to the harbour with its stink of fish, then climbed the hill, hurrying past St Leonard's College with the wind snapping at her skirts, along the length of South Street until she came to her brother's front door. She paused to draw the corner of her shawl over the brass plate bearing his name,

John Adamson M.D. He had spent years away from home, studying and travelling. The plate gave her hope he was here to stay.

Before she could reach for the bell-rope, the door opened and she was nearly bundled into the road by a body coming out. He raised his hat in belated apology, then strode off, hanging on to it in the strengthening breeze. Sir David Brewster, Principal of the University, was a blustering presence on which to hang her worries.

In the lobby she cocked her ear to the voices in the parlour. John's, the gravel on the river floor, and Robert's, the youngest of her brothers, rippling across it. She slipped through the lobby to leave her basket of eggs in the kitchen then went to join them. Robert was in front of the hearth, shifting his weight from one foot to the other. 'Janie, you should have come earlier. Brewster's only just gone.'

She took Rob's arm and drew him away from the fire. She'd spent long enough nursing him through fevers. 'He nearly knocked me over on his way out. And what was he fechting about the day?'

John's smile was slow but infectious. 'No more fechting. He had news from England. The Fox likes the calotypes we sent him. We can go ahead.'

The Fox and The Rooster, she called them, and the boys had liked her joke. Of the two, at least William Henry Fox Talbot was at a distance, holed up in his English den playing with his shadow pictures and writing, writing all the time: letters, books and papers that went to London, to Paris, to his friend in St Andrews, telling Brewster he had discovered how to capture light on paper. Brewster, too busy to perfect the method, had given the task to John. For a year he and Rob had been caught up in a ferment of picture-taking – crouching on street corners, squinting through the eye of their camera, bringing the paper home and persuading it to yield up the shadows hidden in the weave of its fibres.

Jane went to poke the fire. 'What about the patents?'

The Fox was wily. If there was money to be made, it would be his.

John spread his hands. 'He won't take out a patent here, not in Scotland.'

Her brother's skill had won Fox Talbot over. She took Rob's face in her hands. 'There you are then. Robert Adamson, calotyper. When will you put your plate up?'

He shook off her caress. 'Soon, it looks like.'

'And have you found a place?' Jane asked.

Rob's eagerness was as infectious as John's smile. Each week Jane brought in butter and eggs and took back her brothers' news, storing up their latest achievements to think about in the dull days in between. In St Andrews there was always something new in the air. Their eldest brother ran the farm and her mother had a girl to help. If Robert was to set up in business, Jane could keep house for him, do his books, help with his customers. Her mother would be the first to agree that Rob shouldn't be on his own.

John and Rob looked at each other. 'Brewster has heard of a house on the Calton, near Princes Street. The garden faces south, to get the light. Rob could go as soon as he is ready.'

One of the coals sparked and made a fizz on the hearth rug and she went to flick it away. Edinburgh. But it made perfect sense. How many pictures could you take in a wee place like this, perched on its lonely rock above the sea?

'I'll go with him,' John said, 'to see him settled.'

She caught John's eye. 'And after that?' John would come back to his doctoring. Who would look after Rob?

John's look warned her not to put difficulties in Rob's way. 'Och, we'll sort something out.' Rob was interested only in his work. 'Come and see what we've been doing.'

On her way through the lobby she picked up a shawl which she threw over Rob's shoulders.

In the acrid dampness of the wash-house, the chill went

straight to her bones. The window was covered in a red cloth. Trays filled with different solutions blinked at her in the half light, each of them holding a different mystery. Above them, pictures hung on a cord, pegged by their corners like washing on a still day, the kind of day you got at the farm in the lea of the hill, not here in St Andrews where the wind was always from the sea.

These were negatives, the world turned around so that dark was light and light was dark. Soon, by some other method, the dark and the light would be reversed and the picture restored. Something about them caught at her innards, like a parallel world she hadn't known was there.

Beside her, Rob's freckles had faded over the winter, and his hair glinted copper and gold. He went to a drawer and pulled out pictures made the previous week. 'These are what Talbot saw. They're good,' he said, 'aren't they?'

They were pictures of the places she had passed that afternoon, the castle and the Spindle, the towers of the cathedral. And there were portraits too; John's face, narrow and kind, Brewster with his bulbous nose. She couldn't deny there was truth in them, but all of them were trapped in shades of grey or yellow or brown. 'If it's what folk want,' she said.

John, watching from the shadows, sent Rob away to the kitchen to see if there was to be tea. For once he did as he was told and made off down the hall, whistling to himself. She and John went back to the parlour, hearing Rob chaffing the maid in the kitchen and the girl pretending to scold him in return.

John closed the door and drew the curtains to keep out the early dark. 'You're not pleased,' he said.

Jane sighed. Rob had come to St Andrews to find work indoors and so that John could look after him. 'Edinburgh's full of soot and smoke . . .' she said. And much worse, she had heard. Here the relentless wind kept muck from hanging in the air and infection out of the streets.

John shook his head. 'It's what he wants. And he deserves it. He has the talent.'

According to John, Rob was the one who had perfected Talbot's method. He had discovered the part of the process that made the difference. She had misjudged her wee brother, the one they had fussed over all his life.

Something at the window had caught John's eye so that his back was towards her. 'Maybe you should go with him,' Jane forced out the words. She would miss John more than Rob.

John turned on his heels to face her. 'I have plenty to do. And he's a grown man. It's time he struck out.'

Struck out. Which of them other than John had struck out? And he, thank the Lord, had come back.

Rob was at the door with a tea tray. She went to take it from him, giving the cups an angry rattle as she set them on the side table. 'Are there no scones?' she said.

When Rob had come back with a plateful of pancakes, they sat together, slathering them with butter. Rob set down his cup and stretched out his arms and legs.

'Janie thinks you need somebody with you,' John said.

Rob licked a smear of butter off his thumb. John was right, he had found some well of confidence Jane hadn't seen before.

Rob pulled a face. 'John can come and help me find a lens maker. Choosing decent paper might take the longest. Or do you think I won't behave myself?'

Rob had never been one for high jinks. He always had his nose in a book or in some model he'd made just to see if it would work. She couldn't picture him so far from home with only a maid and a housekeeper, neither of whom would notice a change in his colour or listen for the deepening of a cough.

John was settled here. It occurred to neither of them that *she* could be part of Rob's adventure. But why would it? Rob said that it was drudgery to make a calotype, hours of preparing the paper, rinsing the negative, printing and rinsing again. Could she learn to see the ghostly faces, put her hands in the trays of winking water and bring out the magic of light?

'Have you told Mother?' she said.

The men looked at each other. That would be her job.

With the darkness coming in, she said she would stay the night. She slept badly in the cold high-ceilinged room and when sleep finally came there was no crowing of the cock or bark of the collie to waken her so she rose late and took her breakfast alone. Rob had gone to his teaching in the college, John to some meeting with the Provost. She tried to cheer herself with the thought that John would stay here and nothing much would change. But what about Rob? What about herself?

She could be flung like driftwood between the farm and the town, along the coast path or clattering by coach through Boarhills. Or she could be the one to look after him in Auld Reekie, exchange the crumbling ruins for new monuments and marble statues, to stand in a south-facing garden with Edinburgh laid out before her?

Setting off for home, she walked round by the castle. Spring had come early and the ancient walls were taking on a downy coat of moss, the sea keeking in through the gaps. She thought about telling her mother that Rob was even cleverer than they knew and needed to show it. And that Calton Hill was above the sooty air of Edinburgh, not so far from the sea.

Avoiding St Leonards in case she might blunder in and tell The Rooster to take his calotypes back where they had come from, she went down to the harbour by the pier. There were worse things than the stink of fish. She bought half a dozen herring for their dinner.

Ahead of her the bay had lost its green-grey mood and crashed sapphire black against the foot of Kinkell Braes. She knew her Latin and Greek, *Calotype* meant beautiful picture, but if Rob were to make a picture of the sea, it would be only a shadow, nothing like this living thing that sent up rainbow clouds of spray.

CHAPTER THREE

The Restless City

Edinburgh, May 1843

Jessie uncorked the silver solution and watched it flow across the paper, tipping the sheet from side to side. To get an even coating she should have used a brush or a rag. She'd know better next time.

'Whit are you daein'?'

Her hand stayed steady and she let out her breath. 'Nothing, Mother. Just redding up. I'm nearly done.' She was at the wash-stand, away from the light. Her mother could see only shadows.

The idea of the photogram had come from the *Edinburgh Review* and it hadn't taken Jessie long to gather what she needed; paper from the writing desk, silver salts from the apothecary in Rose Street. 'Wear gloves,' he'd said, 'or your fingers will turn black.' The fern, whose lacy fronds she was arranging on the paper, had been easy to find on the north-facing slope of Calton Hill. The final thing she needed was the sun and today she had it in abundance. She must make the most of it.

'Where's May?' the voice was querulous.

'She's ben the room.'

'I want May. She's my daughter, you know.'

'I'm your other daughter, May's sister.'

'Come where I can see you. What do they cry you?'

Jessie removed her gloves and stood close to her mother, laying a hand on her elbow. 'I'm Jessie, mother. Come away now.'

The old woman's eyes were growing more opaque every day. 'I had two daughters. One was bonny, the other was plain. Why can I not go home?'

'Remember, we came to Edinburgh, all of us, after faither died. I'm Jessie.' The skin on her mother's hand was stretched thin over the knuckles. 'We'll go and see May now.'

The magazine had recommended exposing the paper outside but the window sill would have to do. She heaved up the sash window so that not even a smear on the glass would disfigure the sunlight. The ledge was broad and there was no wind. She took a last look at the fern splayed out in the sun and led her mother away.

May was in the lobby with a basket of washing under her arm.

'Mother's greetin' again,' Jessie said. 'It's only you she wants.'

May shifted the weight of the washing. 'She's getting wandered. She doesn't mean it against you.'

The maid could have seen to the washing but on a fine day May liked an excuse to go down to the green. Jessie wished she had thought of it herself. 'When you come back up, I might go and see Sandy.'

'Don't go bringing back any more of his books,' May said. 'We have too many already. Could you go to the baker? We need a loaf.'

Jessie nodded. Sandy, their brother, lived and worked close but every outing was a matter for negotiation. When May had gone, Jessie settled the old woman in her chair and went to find a clean pair of gloves.

From the shoulder of Calton Hill, Jessie could taste the salty edge on the wind that kept the stink of the Old Town at bay.

By the time she had reached Leith Walk, she could make out the gleam of the Forth and behind it the green hills of Fife. Somewhere beyond was Perth with its ring of purple mountains. Her father and a younger brother lay buried there but she no longer thought of it as home. She and May looked after the house in the east end of the New Town, a good flat with high ceilings and room for a lodger. In her younger days she had minded her brothers. Now it was their mother, her mind turning weak as water, who needed minding, keeping Jessie away from the galleries and museums, from walking in the Meadows and the Castle Gardens. Their future was here and one day she would embrace it. In the meantime, she thanked the Lord for Sandy and his magazines.

By the time she was down in Waterloo Place, the air had lost its brightness. At the North Bridge she looked down on Canal Street and across to the Mound. Ahead of her the castle crouched on its rock like a sleeping dragon.

Last week Jessie had gone with her brother to a lecture in the University where they were told the castle rock was a newcomer, thrown up by the eruption of a volcano: the stopper in a bottle emptied of its fizz. She raised her hand and asked the professor, 'Is the castle rock just ash?' The professor leaned forward. He had a high forehead and his eyebrows beetled in a single line across his brow. 'Ash? When lava cools and hardens it makes one of the hardest substances there is. The rock on which our castle stands is *basalt*.' He spat the word out and a drop of his spittle hurtled across the space between the lectern and the front row of listeners. There was laughter but Jessie was unabashed. She had her answer. On their way home, she and Sandy recalled the words of Heraclitus: *panta rhei,* everything must change.

In the lea of the castle, gardens had been planted over the Nor' Loch, the city's old cesspit, a place of bones and bodies, concealing terrible secrets. Now they were talking of bringing the railway in from Haymarket as far as the North Bridge. The folk of the New Town were up in arms at the thought of all that grime stirred up again.

If they wouldn't have the railway, thought Jessie, maybe the dragon would wake and spit out its stopper, leaving the air stained and the view spoiled. The professor would pour scorn on the idea. The basalt wouldn't budge but Edinburgh was still a restless city.

Perched between Princes Street and the valley floor, the monument to Scott was well under way. Masons hung from it like spiders, chapping and chiselling, kicking themselves into position on the raw edges of the stonework. Out in the road, a disturbance made a horse rear. The coachman shouted a curse and passers by scattered from under the plunging hooves. When the commotion had subsided, Jessie stopped to watch the builders, sharing the city's impatience for the spire to be completed. Some things, like the fern on the windowsill, couldn't be hurried.

With dust drying her mouth, she crossed to the north side of Princes Street where she noticed two men pushing a handcart. She would have taken them for engineers, but instead of going over to the building works, they stopped at the corner of Hanover Street, took off their coats, and set about unloading. The younger man, fair-skinned and jumpy as a flea, took down a four-legged stand and stood it beside him. The other screwed a box to the top of it, raised his eyes to the sky and frowned. Older than the first, he bore a family resemblance. 'The light's good,' he said. We may as well give it a try. Tell me when you're ready for the paper.'

Jessie had already come to a halt. The younger man saw her interest and nodded a greeting, granting her permission to stay and watch.

The box had a rounded end which he pointed at the monument. The older of the two passed a square frame to his companion who inserted it into the back of the box and covered the entire contraption in a black cloth.

It was the first time Jessie had seen a camera for making a picture like the one she was making with her fern. She watched as they removed the cover from the protruding lens. While its owner tapped out a nervous rhythm with his fingers, the other stood by with a stop-watch. 'That's it!' he shouted.

Jessie's head was full of questions. How had they treated the paper? What made their picture so much quicker than her photogram? Could they do it when the light was poor? Just as she was stepping forward to ask, a crowd of six or seven ministers came flapping round the corner, birling her into the road. She was only saved from going under the wheels of a cart by the last of the group, the only one to have seen her predicament. He led her to the safety of a shop door and by the time he had apologised for the clumsiness of his friends, the men with the camera had moved away.

Jessie accepted the minister's apology. 'I could see you had a lot to talk about.'

His cassock had the impenetrable blackness of new worsted and his face wore the earnestness of youth. He frowned. 'I think we've talked enough. Now we need to show our mettle.'

This was the week of the Assembly when the Kirk looked likely to split in two. Jessie guessed her young saviour was part of the schism but it didn't do to jump to conclusions

'And who are you for?' she asked.

'For Chalmers.' Seeing her smile, he stammered a correction. 'For the Free Kirk, for the right to choose our own minister, not have one forced on us by the gentry.'

'Good,' she said, dusting off her frock, 'That puts us on the same side.'

He nodded as he left. 'May the Lord help us in our cause.'

She watched him go. In two days' time the Kirk would make its decision and she had no doubt he would be with the dissenters. How many of the older men with settled families and comfortable stipends would walk away from their old lives? The young had the least to lose.

As the street settled back to its usual business, Jessie couldn't help but notice that the door where she had taken shelter was flanked by windows filled with prints of highland scenes. There was something familiar about them and she looked for the name above the door. *Alexander Hill, Printer and Stationer.* In the mellow-stoned elegance of Edinburgh's New Town, the heather hills of Perthshire stepped suddenly closer.

In his office, Sandy laughed at the story of the minister who worshipped Thomas Chalmers. 'All the same, it looks like the Disruption will come off.'

Although she shared Sandy's hope, she couldn't ignore the tug of sadness for things lost. Their minister was for the established Kirk. Their family had pledged to Chalmers. There would be no going back to their pew in Greenside Church.

'So where will we go, come Sunday?'

'They say the Glenorchy Chapel will have us.'

Jessie pictured herself leaving the house on Sunday morning with her mother and May, turning the other way at the end of the road. Her father had always said changes were lightsome, but some came harder than others.

Sandy had put aside two new magazines for her. 'How are your experiments coming on?' He knew about her efforts with the photogram. She told him how close she was to making one. 'What I'd really like to have is a camera. I saw two folk just now, brothers by the look of them, taking pictures of the Monument.'

Sandy frowned. 'A daguerrotype, you mean?'

Jessie had seen a picture held in a copper plate, shining like a jewel, too dear for most folk to contemplate.

'No,' she said. 'They were using paper. I heard them say so.'

Sandy shook his head. 'So much to read these days. I must have missed it.'

Every new discovery brought more in its wake, some arriving with as much noise and kerfuffle as the train from Glasgow, others creeping in while nobody was watching.

Jessie picked up the magazines. Sandy had work to do. On her way out she remembered she had something to ask him.

'That stationers, opposite the Institution. Would it be the same Hills we knew in Perth?'

Sandy looked up from a bundle of letters he was untying. 'Oh aye. Alexander gets all the work his brother puts his way. They've done very well for themselves.'

Alexander's brother, David, had left Perth to be a limner, a painter of scenery, and his family had followed him. He was famous now but Jessie could still see his gallus smile lighting up the dim closes of the Watergate on a summer evening and hear his laughter at some joke of his own making.

At home, she went to the scullery, laid down the loaf and lifted the lid off the soup pot. The barley had started to swell. She added water to the mutton stock whose damp and meaty aroma filled the air.

May appeared with the first load of washing from the green, the muslin and the thin cambric dry enough to have its creases shaken out.

'How has she been?' Jessie said.

May sighed. 'She has taken to wandering. I was watching from the scullery and saw her on the back green.' She pulled a blackened paper from her pinnie pocket. 'I'm sorry. I found her throwing this on the midden. It's that picture you had on the window, isn't it?'

Setting down the basket she handed Jessie the crumpled sheet.

Jessie smoothed the paper. The surface, for all it was cracked and dry, had kept the image of the fern. Its whorls were dim but discernible. It was hardly a thing of beauty, but the exact shape of it, the number of fronds and the curve of each spray was captured in every detail.

'Look!' she said.

May mistook her excitement for annoyance. 'Can you no do another one?'

She could but it hardly mattered. She had only wanted to know it could be done, that the sun could work its magic, not just for professors or gentry with time on their hands but for her, Jessie Mann, on her mother's window-sill.

The Disruption, a strange name for an act of faith, was greater than anybody hoped. Neither Jessie nor May were in George Street when the ministers took their long walk to Tanfield but the city and the country knew that four hundred men had left to form the Free Kirk.

The walk to Glenorchy was shorter but no less of a wrench. May and Jessie steered their mother, *where are ye takin' me, this isna'e the way,* along a pavement thronged with silent worshippers. At the chapel, it looked like half of Edinburgh had made the same choice and it was a struggle to pick out Sandy in the crowd.

Inside, folk moved along the pews to let newcomers in. Standing shoulder to shoulder, Jessie lent her voice to the psalms and watched motes of sunlight made red, blue and yellow by the stained glass saints. Was its rich artistry an affront to the ministers who had become poor overnight? Well, if needs be they could take the glass out and sell it. Until then, she would enjoy its jewelled brightness, be grateful for the freedom of choice and vow not to be impatient at what felt like her captivity.

May half disapproved of her guddling with silver salts, *interfering in nature* she called it and said, like their old minister, that there had to be a choice between science and religion. Sandy disagreed. God made the world in seven days, he said. In another thousand years they still wouldn't know every wonder of it but that needn't stop them trying to find out.

After the sermon, outside in the caller air, the minister shook each worshipper by the hand. While Sandy and May caught up with a group of old friends, Jessie's eye was drawn to a man of her own age, straight-backed and with a fine head of hair escaping from under his hat. As if sensing Jessie's eyes on him, he turned to look and after a moment's puzzlement came over to speak. His open smile erased the years that had passed since she'd last laid eyes on him.

He took off his hat. 'Mrs Mann? And Jessie, surely!'

She touched her mother's arm. 'Mother, it's David Hill. From Perth, remember?'

Her mother clutched at a tendril of memory. 'Tom Hill's son? Did he no go away to Edinburgh?'

David Hill always knew the right thing to say. 'He did indeed!' He stepped back as if it would help her mother see him better and spread his arms. 'And look, he is still here! Although his faither is long gone, I'm afraid.' He held out his hand to Jessie. 'I heard you'd moved south. I don't know how I haven't seen you before.'

They exchanged a few words about the service and the Disruption. Twenty years, it must be that, had done him no harm and he looked the world in the eye as he always had.

'I see Edinburgh suits you,' she said.

He plucked at his sleeve and said it did, although not everything had gone well, his wife Ann having died two years since.

'I'm sorry for your loss. She was a bonny lassie.'

He dropped his eyes then raised them again. 'She was, and had the bonniest voice for a song. Luckily for me,' the smile was restored, 'she left her likeness behind. My wee girl, Chattie. You should come and see us. We have a lot to catch up on.'

They were in Inverleith, he said, and they should come next Sunday afternoon. Jessie knew the street, new houses near the Botanics. Sandy was right, he had done well for himself.

'And are you going to Tanfield?' he asked. 'I for one want to see it.'

In the following week, the dissenting ministers would reconvene to sign a Deed of Demission, their pledge to the new Kirk.

Jessie frowned. 'Is it not just the ministers?'

'I think there will be many more besides. All the supporters. Let's hope there's plenty of room.'

After he replaced his hat and walked away, Sandy and May rejoined them.

'That was a laddie from Perth,' her mother told them. 'His name slips my mind.'

At the end of that same week, on a clear morning, Jessie was taking a walk up Calton Hill, thinking she would look for another fern, when she saw the camera set on the grassy verge, its young owner standing over it. He could have been twenty but looked younger. Something in the set of his shoulders and the way his hair was parted on the left caught at her heart. Her youngest brother's name was rarely mentioned but sometimes Jessie felt him close by, watching her in her new life.

The laddie nodded to her then went back to studying his watch.

'You will soon have pictures of the whole of Edinburgh,' she said.

He answered without looking up. 'Only if the sun stays with us.'

She watched as he covered his lens and removed the picture from the camera, keeping it out of the light.

'Tell me,' she said. 'How does it happen so quickly?'

He was unsurprised at her interest. 'Fox Talbot, an Englishman, found a way to develop the latent image.'

In his ready grin there was delight in having somebody to share the knowledge he'd worked so hard to master. 'The picture forms quickly,' he said. 'If the sun is strong, less than a minute. If the weather's dull, maybe three. Either way, we have to coax it out of the paper.'

Jessie nodded. Some other day she would find out how the coaxing was done.

She'd meant to climb up to the Observatory but this

44

conversation was more to her liking than admiring the view from the top of the hill. As he packed up the apparatus and turned back down the hill, she fell into step beside him.

'You've lost your helper,' she said.

'My brother's away home now. He was just seeing me settled in.' Home, he said was St Andrews.

'Do you miss it?'

He frowned before he answered. 'I don't think about it.'

She could believe it. Bent over his camera, he thought of nothing but the chemistry of light.

When he came to a gate set in the wall at the side of the path he stopped and searched his pockets until he found a printed card and handed it to her.

'Tell anybody you think might be interested,' he said. 'I can do portraits too. You should come and see. Have one done yourself.'

The gate swung closed behind him, creaking on its hinges. Rock House had stood empty for months. Jessie read the card and saw it had become home to Robert Adamson, Calotypist. She put the card in her sleeve, savouring the word on her tongue.

In David Hill's house in Inverleith Row, Jessie stood next to the tall parlour windows admiring the white plaster cornice and the view of the walled garden. David stood beside her. Sandy and May were settled in two fine armchairs next to the unlit fire.

'Over there,' David pointed to the garden wall, 'are the new gardens. Princes Street's only a mile. We're very lucky to be here.'

The pause let them all remember the gap left by a mother and a wife.

'How do you manage?' May asked.

'Chattie's with my sister most of the time. She's fine company, but I have too many other places to be.'

He came away from the window, as if he saw only regrets through its square panes, and invited Jessie to a brocade couch with polished wooden arms where he sat down beside her. His wee girl had enticed their mother away to see the rest of the house. In the distance their voices could be heard, sharing a child-like interest in the contents of each room and in each other.

Sandy stretched out his legs. 'Did you go to the signing? I hear Tanfield was full to bursting.'

David nodded then rested his chin on one hand, cast into deep thought. 'The sight of it has stayed with me ever since. Sic a thing to see, four hundred men pledging themselves to the Free Kirk. And nearly as many onlookers as ministers. If you'd been there, you would have felt the weight of it.' He went on, talking almost to himself, rehearsing some argument going on in his mind. 'Just being there moved me, but there was more to it than that. I felt there was some purpose in it for me as well as for the Kirk. I've been wondering ever since what it might be and can think of only one thing.'

His gaze was on Sandy, although from the look in his eye, Jessie guessed that in his heart he was talking to somebody else.

'I'm going to see Chalmers tomorrow to tell him I'll paint it for him, for the Kirk. A Disruption Painting. If they'll let me.'

The footsteps close by of the bairn and the old woman made the silence in the room more profound. Sandy leaned forward in the armchair. 'That'll be a gey big painting.'

David nodded and gave a rueful smile. 'It's the only way folk who couldn't be there will be able to see it for themselves. The Kirk will have to pay me for the privilege, but they can sell copies to parishes. To anybody who wants one.'

Jessie thought they were sure to agree, Chalmers and the Moderator. The artist's intention was a noble thing – as great as the dimensions of the picture he was planning to paint.

'It does you credit,' she says, 'to have thought of it. To want to do it.'

David Hill held his hands in front of him and turned them so the palms were upward, fingers outstretched. 'If I can do it well enough. Remember, I'm a painter of landscapes.'

His hair was peppered with grey and as they had stood by the window, Jessie had seen the shadows under his eyes. He already had a full and busy life yet here he was determined to add to his labours.

The walls around them were hung with Highland scenes. Jessie's eye was drawn to a small portrait of his wife, above the piano.

'A bonny thing but not by me,' he said, following her eyes. 'I never took to portraiture. The faces of four hundred ministers won't come easy.'

May frowned. 'Chalmers and the leaders . . . they'll have to be recognisable . . . but not every minister? Surely you can't paint the likeness of all of them?'

He shook his head. 'May Mann, think what you're saying! Every minister has played his part. All are equal in the eyes of God. How could I paint one as himself and another as a cipher, some kind of everyman?'

'I was only thinking of the work,' May said.

This made him laugh. 'You're right. It's no small task. It will fill my time for a year, I'm sure. Maybe more.'

The more she heard, the more Jessie understood the scale of the undertaking. Her weekly attendance at church and an offering in the collection plate hardly compared.

The door opened and their mother came in, hand in hand with the bairn. 'This wee soul has had me all over the house,' she said. 'I could fair do with a cup.'

Chattie hopped from one foot to the other. 'It's tea-time, Dada!'

He went over and kneeled down beside her. 'Well, call to Nettie and let's see what we can do.'

'So when will you start on the painting?' Jessie said when tea had been poured.

'They'll have to collect up the ministers before they go home and send them to me straight away. Before I as much as lift a brush, I've four hundred sketches to make.'

Barely a week had passed when the news went round that Mr Hill of the Royal Scottish Academy had enlisted the help of the calotypist from St Andrews. If Jessie had gone to Rock House and sat for a calotype portrait, maybe she would have made the connection. But as was the case with her half-completed photogram, in the end it made no difference. The artist would be saved the work of sketching and the ministers waiting to sit for him could go home and start their new lives.

When Jessie heard this, her heart fluttered in her breast. She knew what could happen when things were brought together; heat and rock, sun and silver. Something or somebody had brought together the artist, the Kirk and the calotypist: three chemicals thrown in a dish where they might lie still and fail to combine or bubble into new life.

She found excuses to walk on Calton Hill but never saw Robert Adamson. He was in his grey house or behind the high walls of its garden, kept busy by the line of ministers trooping up the front steps in a procession that never seemed to end, as if the one in front, after making his visit, simply walked back round to join the end of the queue.

'I saw Thomas Chalmers there the day,' she told May a week or two later. 'The ministers have taken to the calotypes.'

'Ministers are the least of their troubles,' May said. 'Yon Adamson has all of Edinburgh at his door.'

In the afternoon, Jessie walked around the hill. From a carriage drawn up below Rock House, two men alighted and after them a woman in a red silk frock with a wide lace collar. The men looked up to the sky, shading their eyes, as if they possessed the knowledge of exactly how much sun was needed for a calotype picture. Ministers were hardly known for going about in private carriages. Whatever Adamson had hatched, David Hill had lent it wings.

The next day their mother fell on the stairs and took to her bed where she lay with her face turned to the wall, refusing to eat.

Jessie could see her days of minding were coming to an end. When next she stood on the North Bridge and looked down to the valley floor, she imagined it furrowed by railway lines and sensed the rumble of trains beneath her feet.

CHAPTER FOUR

The Bird of Wax

Amelia Paton, Dunfermline, July 1843

When Mr Hill first came to our door, I was up in the studio with a nugget of wax in my hand. I don't remember how I came to be holding it, only that the sketch I'd been working on was not going well and when I held the wax I felt something in the heart of it, maybe the blackbird at the window singing the end of the day or a maybe a darting swift.

Hearing the artist arrive, I hurried downstairs. My mother had lectured me on how he was a relative and how much help he could be to my brother who was in London, trying his hand as a painter. That was in the morning, as she unlocked the linen press. We had a maid for making beds but the laying out of linen was a ritual and only the best would do for the visitor. It was the summer before last, five years since I had put up my hair and two years since Mr Hill's wife had died.

On the doorstep, the artist's face was in shadow as he shook each of our hands. His bairn wriggled beside him like a tadpole. Her name was Chattie and her wee face was white with tiredness. Although I was never one for minding bairns, my heart went out to her. When I bent down to speak, she unwound herself from his legs and I took her away for some milk though I would rather have stayed and heard what her father had to say.

Later we sat in the parlour where a last glimmer of sun threw the lines of his face into relief. I couldn't say how much of a mark his wife's death had made on him but I did see some light in his eye for his life still to come. He had brought my father a copy of his *Land of Burns* which pleased Joseph greatly. 'These lithographers are canny,' he said. 'A picture can be reproduced as many times as folk will buy it.'

The artist's smile flashed white in the gloaming. Lithography, he said, was only the half of it. He was starting a great painting to commemorate the recent disruption of the Kirk and instead of preparing sketches of the ministers, he had found a partner to help him make pictures using only the light of the sun. This interested my father more than any trouble amongst ministers and he asked about how it was done. 'Always something new to keep us on our toes,' he said, as he tapped his pipe on the fender.

Next morning, the men were away to see the new weaving sheds at St Leonards where my father designs jacquard linen. Chattie, said Mr Hill, could go with them but my mother frowned. 'There is too much noise and stoor down there for a bairn. Amelia can mind her.'

I thought of my bird and how I could fashion the tail of a swift but I knew that down the New Row, weavers who had no work slouched and spat at gentry passing by. I agreed and Chattie jiggled about until her father said she could stay behind.

The sunlight tempted me out of doors so I took her through the hedge at the back of the garden to the burn. There I told her to take off her stockings and shoes and I hung on to her skirt as she leaned out over the bank to look for minnows and sticklebacks. She was so eager in her leaning, I worried she would fall in and soak herself. 'Come away now,' I said. 'We'll go back and make daisy chains.'

Her father found us in the garden, my fingers green from splitting stalks and Chattie's pinnie smeared with pollen. She ran to him and he lifted her onto the stone bench. He had picked a buttercup from the grass and held it under her chin, then under his, showing her how it shone a yellow light on the pale underskin. They made such a bonny picture, I ached to recreate it.

Our house is full to bursting with paintings and other antiques and that day, as every other, we sat down to our mince and tatties under a ceiling of prancing cherubs. I watched Chattie gaze at their plump legs and cheeks as we talked of my brother's progress. 'Amelia has a good eye, too,' my mother said, 'and is very conscientious with her drawing.'

'I'm sure she is,' replied Mr Hill, with the politeness due to the daughter of his host. I held my tongue but in the afternoon my mother announced, 'We should go to the abbey. It's a fine subject for one of Mr Hill's landscapes. And Amelia can keep him company.'

I was brought up to be in awe of nobody but Mr Hill was at the forefront of Scottish painters and Secretary to the Edinburgh academy. I thought of my grey and flimsy sketches and the blackbird (or the swift) still waiting.

At the abbey, my mother and father took Chattie for a walk in the woods, leaving the artist and me together on the path beneath the ancient buttresses. He had an easel lent by my father and I had a sketching book. He pinned up a sheet and flexed his fingers. 'Are you not going to join me? Or are you wearied of a view you can see any day?'

A thought swooped down and spoke in my ear. Were my parents planning more than an acquaintance between their daughter and the widowed artist? I was robbed of my tongue. While his strokes with the charcoal grew smooth and masterful, the call of my still unmade blackbird was muted by the gurgle of the burn in the glen and the softening solitude around us.

'Are you a romantic, Amelia, or do you prefer to paint people rather than nature in your own work?'

He stood away from his composition. In it the walls were if

52

anything higher and more forbidding than I saw them. It reminded me of all those engravings where a lord or peasant surveys a distant scene. In the contemplation of art, I lost my shyness.

'Would a figure add to the composition?'

He raised his eyebrows and nodded to himself. I had surprised him. 'I think it would.'

Then he had me stand in a pool of dappled sunlight, looking up at the louring walls. I would be the figure he needed.

With not a single cloud to dim the warmth of the sun, I soon felt my neck prickle with heat and in the simmering stillness I could easily have taken off my shoes and stockings and planted my feet in the cool and twiggy soil, like Chattie by the burn.

'What would I be thinking, standing here?' I said, trying to model for him as best I could.

The flash of white teeth again. 'What do you think, Amelia? Is there a prince coming through those woods behind us? Or a dragon waiting to be slain?'

I liked the sound of my name on his lips and I was growing into the part he had chosen for me.

Back at home, I agreed to my mother's suggestion to assemble some old portrait sketches for him to look at, should he ask. At night I lay awake, bothered by an itch on my neck, failing to untangle my thoughts from a skein of princes and maidens.

Next morning he was in the studio, casting his eye over my portraits. He is not the tallest of men but he cast a long shadow in the room. My mother beckoned me in from the doorway.

He looked up from his considering. 'I would like to see more lady artists in our exhibition,' he said. 'If you send us something next spring, I'd be happy to look at it.'

The light shifted. I was the lady artist. My mother had only the keys to the linen press.

All winter I worked at my portraits. Aunts, cousins, visitors were persuaded to sit for me while my mother regaled them with the visit of our cousin the artist, his affability, his bairn, his being, as far as she knew, alone. I continued after they had gone. Only when the chill was in my bones did I lay down the powdery charcoal and bring the life back to my fingers by working at a new nugget of wax.

Come the spring my work was rewarded. My brother was not the only one to have a picture in the Academy exhibition and my father declared we would all go to Edinburgh to celebrate his bairns' success.

A chill wind blew down Hanover Street that day and through the grand portico of the great gallery. I had thought Mr Hill would come to meet us but there was no sign of him. Inside, my mother and father paid polite respect to my spidery drawings, displayed in a modest corner. My brother's canvas, full of colour and exuberance, had a whole wall to itself. Here was a painter the world would admire. I saw my ambition for what it was – a girl's foolish pride.

I trailed through the other rooms still hoping to come upon my mentor. Instead I found *Dunfermline Abbey*, the painting he had made from his sketch that summer's day. My father joined me there and nodded his approval. 'She has your figure,' he said.

But the lassie in the clearing had her hair still down her back. I had been only a reference for shadow and scale, an excuse for an artistic flourish.

Joseph knew my spirits were low. 'Come away and see the calotypes,' he said.

Mr Hill's sun pictures were thought by some to equal Rembrandt in their beauty but in the panelled room where brooding ministers looked down on us, I couldn't warm to their severity.

'Not these,' said Joseph and drew me to where another calotype was framed, of Mr Hill and Chattie on his knee, his arm tight around her and a glimmer of that elfin smile in her eyes. It was the picture I had seen that day in the garden, the one I wanted to paint and never would.

'Now that's a bonny thing,' my father said.

It was indeed. It spoke of truth and tenderness, more so than any romantic notion or girlish fancy. I was outdone not by an artist, but by a fragment of light.

Now I check the linen press each day and walk to the mill sheds to take my father his piece. On the New Row, I hold my head high when the weavers jostle my elbow

I have added to my birds of wax and made some birds of clay. They stand in a row on a shelf under the skylight, some plumped and preening, some with their beaks open, ready to sing. None of them has spread its wings.

CHAPTER FIVE

The Charm of the Man

Elizabeth Rigby, Edinburgh, September 1843

Within a year of our leaving Norfolk and arriving in Edinburgh, we were witness to the great Disruption of the Scottish Kirk, an event which greatly vexed the citizens of our new abode. As Episcopalians, we stood apart from this furore, and I remember it now only for the part it played in bringing us to the door of Mr D.O. Hill, the artist who was to make such an impression on me as a writer, a thinker, and, I freely admit, as a woman.

Of course, what brought us together was not the Kirk itself or any of its black-frocked martyrs, but the artist's much heralded facility with the art of the calotype. As both a student and critic of painting, I was sceptical of this so-called advance. Nature and Art are inextricably intertwined but the artist must have the upper hand. A mechanical drawing (I had observed a friend using the *camera lucida*) could never emulate the artistry of the soul.

I couldn't deny, however, a certain curiosity about Mr Hill, whose name was bandied more and more at the gatherings we attended. When Mamma announced that she and our dear friend, Lady Drysdale, were intent on having a calotype made, I consented to join them on their visit to the artist's studio on Calton Hill, only a short walk from our own accommodation.

When Mr Hill himself opened the door to us, my fears for a dull afternoon were quickly allayed. I still consider Mr Lockhart the most handsome of my acquaintances, but Mr Hill's countenance was so pleasing and his manner so amiable I began to anticipate a visit of more than scientific interest!

In the parlour, where tea was served, he spoke to my mother for some time about what had brought us to Edinburgh, how we were finding the city and which friends we had in common. This solicitude surprised me since we understood the artist to be a very busy man with many people to see in the course of a day and I must have exhibited some small impatience. He turned his gaze on me and said, 'I hope you're in no hurry, Miss Rigby. A calotype may take a short time but it is still a portrait and no artist would make a start before getting to know something of his sitter.'

I felt foolish for doubting his artistic integrity and may even have blushed when he added, with all his natural grace, 'And of course the chance to talk with people like yourselves adds to the pleasure of the enterprise.'

To conceal my embarrassment I agreed vociferously with his approach to portraiture and added, 'Although I myself find capturing the human face stretches my talent to its limit.'

I would have gone on to describe my sketches of Estonia but he was leaning forward and regarding me with new intensity. 'You're an artist?' I nodded and he ran his hand through his hair which settled back in less order than it had been before. 'And one after my own heart,' he said. 'My own difficulties with portraiture were what brought me to the calotype.'

He went on to explain how he had intended to use the 'sun pictures' only as sketches but had become so 'beguiled by their subtle character' (I think these were his words) that he had begun to see them as works of art in their own right.

Lady Drysdale broke into our conversation. 'Most of

Edinburgh agrees with you,' she said, 'judging by the difficulty of making an appointment.'

At this he merely smiled. 'We are never short of work. So perhaps we should make a start.'

His studio was a paved courtyard facing south, where a young man introduced as Mr Adamson was preparing the apparatus.

'I must sit outside?' Mamma asked.

I had read a paper by Mr Fox Talbot and knew enough of this enterprise to explain. 'A calotype requires as much natural light as possible, Mamma.'

'Yes,' said Mr Hill, and I caught a nod of approval directed at me, 'I'm afraid the sun will be in your eyes, Mrs Rigby, but you won't be troubled for long.'

Mr Hill placed mother in what he said would be the best position, chatting with her all the while so that she remained still while Adamson, as far as I understood, timed the making of the picture in the camera.

Next to sit was Lady Drysdale. Then Mr Hill beckoned to me.

'Last but not least,' said Lady Drysdale, who is not beyond a dry wit. The gleam in her eye referred to the fact that I am the tallest girl in any company. Mr Hill, however, was too gallant to respond to this jibe and asked if the two ladies might like to rest indoors while he completed my calotype, a suggestion I found more than welcome, affording me the chance to get to know him away from the regard of others.

When they had left the courtyard, he took away the straight backed chair and brought out a chaise longue from the corner of the yard. Leading me to it, he gave close attention to how best I should arrange myself, altering the folds of my dress and suggesting a change in the angle of my arm.

To cover my awkwardness at this unexpected proximity and to erase Lady Drysdale's remark, I said, 'I wasn't sure there would be time for all of us to sit.'

The artist looked up from his ministrations. 'Luckily the sun has stayed with us,' he said. 'And in any case,' here he turned to his friend, 'I always save the best 'til last. Isn't that so, Robert?'

While Adamson's response was lost in the black cloth under which he was labouring, Mr Hill, as I still thought of him then, gave me a look of such merriment that I put my hand over my mouth to stop my own laughter.

When the exposure was done, we were left entirely alone, but instead of escorting me inside, he drew up a chair next to me, saying I was clearly well-informed about all matters artistic and that he would appreciate my views on the calotypes when they were made. In return I told him of my association with the *Review* and its publisher and editor which he found of immediate interest. We eked out our conversation a little longer, discovering a shared love of Sir Walter Scott. Although I could not match his joy in the poems of Burns, I rejoined my companions in the knowledge I had found a kindred spirit and, despite my enduring scepticism, thought I should give consideration to whatever pictures were produced.

During the walk back to Bernard Crescent, Lady Drysdale informed us of Mr Hill's situation: his reputation as a landscape painter, his position as Secretary to the Scottish Academy and the sad loss of his wife, leaving him with a young daughter to look after.

'At such an early age,' Mother said. 'I could see that house lacked a woman's touch.'

'Oh he doesn't live there,' Lady Drysdale said, 'although it's where he's most often to be found.'

Although it sometimes pains me there are not more women engaged in art and letters, I have always been ready to join in the company of men, especially those who make attentive and chivalrous partners. However I had learned the value of my freedom as a single woman, freedom to write, to travel and to paint. After the unnecessary fracas over my unchaperoned visits to Mr Lockhart, which were of a purely intellectual nature, I was more than ever determined not to sacrifice such freedom for the sake of a marriage which would almost certainly curb my own ambitions. I therefore took no interest in Mr Hill's living arrangements.

The next event was the arrival a few days later of our calotype prints with which Mamma professed herself very well pleased. However, I thought the light and shade more effective in her lined countenance, framed as it was by a bonnet. Though the pose the artist had chosen successfully disguised my stature, my own face had a moonish look, exacerbated by the need to cast down my eyes in the glare of sunlight. All the same I could see in these renditions something beyond the mechanical and was moved to send one picture to Mr Murray with a note remarking on its qualities.

Matilda, my sister, was also impressed. 'Why will anyone need a painter now?' she said. She was regretting her decision not to have visited Rock House and Mamma was ready to comply with her suggestion we go back.

'I think it would do no harm,' she said, 'to call again and have more pictures made. Elizabeth . . . you and he were so congenial, I take it you'll come?'

Mamma of course would have liked all of us 'settled,' but if I was suspicious of her motives for going back to Rock House, my heart still lifted at the prospect of another afternoon in the company of its amiable host. How unsettling it was to be at the mercy of emotions when the intellect was counseling otherwise.

On our second visit we were let in by a housekeeper and asked to wait in the parlour. Two ministers of the church already sat at either side of the unlit fire, deep in conversation. Apparently Mr Hill was still engaged in portraits for the Kirk and it would be some time before we were called. I had time to look around, noting a bound edition of *The Antiquary* on a side table with the latest copy of the *Review*. It seemed the artist was more than at home here. As Mamma and Matilda discussed the calotyping adventure about to take place, I saw poking out from under the magazine a scrap of paper with a rough drawing of a child on it with a line of speech emanating from the mouth. I remembered the daughter and thought this an oddly private thing to be left on view in this austere room.

Soon Mr Hill (if anything he was more handsome than I remembered) swept in, saying his appointment book was clear for the day so he was at our disposal for whatever we had in mind. When Mamma raised her eyebrows, he laughed and said we would begin with a calotype.

When this had been done, with compliments on our choice of dress and questions about our recent engagements, he asked if we would like Mr Adamson to show us the process of developing. Mamma and Matilda were enthusiastic and Mr Adamson, keeping his precious negatives closely wrapped, led us through the house to a back yard. Opposite stood an outhouse with an open door and, as we grew closer, we were met by a strange odour, sharp enough to make me draw back from the threshold.

Mr Adamson smiled at my expression. 'It's just the hypo,' he said. 'It does no harm as long as we leave the window open.'

'The fixing solution,' explained Mr Hill who hung back to accompany me. 'I don't like the smell either, but I think that's because of my ignorance of all the chemicals we have out here.'

I was surprised at this and, as the others went inside, we lingered in the courtyard. 'I imagined you an expert on how a calotype is made.'

He threw back his head, laughing freely before confessing, 'I'm in Robert's workshop most days but in all my life I doubt I'll ever understand what goes on there.'

'You don't help with the developing?'

He folded his arms and let out a sigh. 'I look at the negative and judge if it's worthy of printing. Sometimes we make slight alterations along the way. But all this,' he waved at the door in front of us, 'is Greek to me.'

I was puzzled and also flattered he thought to confide in me. '*Timeo Danaos*,' I said, without thinking, *I fear the Greeks,* although the proverb had no particular relevance.

He finished it for me. '*Et dona ferentes.* Beware Greeks bearing gifts. Well said, Miss Rigby!'

My resolve to remain aloof broke down. 'Please, call me Elizabeth,' I said.

He inclined his head with an upward look from those sparkling eyes. 'Very well, Elizabeth. And since my friends call me D.O., you must do the same.' With this he took my arm to lead me back to the parlour.

With the topic of the sun pictures put aside, we were free to quiz each other more closely on our likes and dislikes, our achievements and ambitions in art. I asked if he was allowing the calotypes to lead him away from his painting, to which he objected with vigour. The camera, he explained, was the helpmate of the artist and even if it was capable of more than he had expected, his principal work was his landscape painting and the commissions it brought him. On top of this was the painting for the Free Kirk which was likely to take up his time for the foreseeable future. I said I was glad to hear this and asked how far he had got.

His expression became less jaunty. 'I've been working on some small studies.' He held out his hands, palms upwards, in a rather affecting gesture of supplication. 'But you see how busy I am.'

Despite this protestation he gave no signal I should leave until the voices of Mamma and Matilda, returning from what I would always think of as the laboratory, brought our conversation to an end.

From that time on, we were invited to Rock House from time to time and I accepted, calling sometimes with Mamma and Matilda, other times alone. Of course the place was his workplace rather than his home and however animated our discussions, there was never the slightest impropriety between us.

In winter a change came over the city. The locals call it *dreich*, meaning grey or gloomy, which is accurate enough for all but a few days when the sea-mist is chased away by a fierce east wind.

With the sun too low on the horizon for making pictures of reliable quality, Adamson, a steady worker who rarely shared our conversations, took himself to his family home in Fife. Mamma fell prey to a bad cold which kept her indoors but saw no harm in my calling on D.O. in what I thought of as his mountain lair. We continued to argue over his calotypes, with or without the presence of other visitors, which I admit I saw progressing all the time in subtlety of effect and composition.

One day he asked for my advice in choosing prints for the Exhibition opening in the spring.

'You will show the calotypes?'

He flashed his smile. 'Yes. They are becoming famous, you know!'

I was aware of a number of articles making favourable mention of the calotypes but was still surprised at their acceptance by the Scottish Academy. It occurred to me this was a turning point and when he led me to the back parlour where several framed pictures were propped up, I said as much.

He nodded in a thoughtful way as if all of this was still a surprise to him. He was standing at my elbow and leaned closer towards me as we surveyed his work.

'What about you, Elizabeth. Are you going to surrender to them now?' he said.

I had to smile at his perspicacity and his way of overcoming my resistance to his sun pictures. I said I would hold out a little longer, wondering if he read into this the same meaning as did I.

By the time Spring and Mr Adamson returned, my obduracy over the calotypes was at an end and on many days I arrived at Rock House just to see who was sitting and what they made of my friends and their new art. I remember Lady Ruthven's refusal to face the camera and how dear D.O., seeing her obstinacy, made the best of it, producing a most original portrait albeit with her back to the camera. I also began to take part in tableaux we judged worthy of a calotype, posing as an allegorical or historical figure and even acquainted myself with some of Robert's dark arts, turning over in my mind how I might write something one day on this still novel subject, perhaps pre-empting London writers less well-versed.

Private moments with D.O., however, became fewer, circumscribed not only by his appointments at the Academy but also by a great deal more activity at Rock House where Miss Mann, a family friend, came almost daily to help with the printing of negatives.

In the afternoons, Charlotte often appeared, brought by his sister Mary who looked after her much of the time and I admit I grew to resent the opening of the front door at three o'clock and her footsteps skittering through to the kitchen where the cook or Miss Mann would distract her. I came to watch too for the restlessness which overtook him once she was back in the house.

'Do you think she might be happier living with your sister?' I once asked him.

He gave a rueful smile. 'Maybe she would. But I would be lost without her.'

I was bemused at this, thinking about all the calls on his time and how freely he gave it. He was friends, I knew, with doctors, engineers, architects and churchmen, all of whom relied on his support. This as much as anything endeared him to me and made me feel that there might be a place in his life for a long legged girl with an enquiring mind, even if I didn't know what that place might be.

All the while Mamma said nothing about how it was between us, asking only after each visit if I had enjoyed our conversations. I always answered Yes, describing the topics we had covered or the tableaux we had worked on with Adamson. I did not mention those moments when, lying on the chaise or arranging myself in the manner of some Greek nymph, D.O. brushed his hand on my shoulder or smoothed a lock of hair.

One day in particular sticks in my mind. Adamson had left us to get on with his developing and D.O. was arranging my dress across my legs for another picture when he asked if I could move my hands across my breast as if in prayer.

Feeling a little tremulous in my movements I said, 'Like this?'

At which he smiled, laid his hands on mine and pressed them closer against my bodice with a look on his face I could hardly bear to return although every part of me wanted to.

He leaned towards me. My hand was on its way to his face and my lips were more than ready to be kissed when a tap on the door sent him hurtling away from me as if propelled by an electrical current.

'Can we come in?' It was Jessie Mann's voice, followed by Chattie's childish wail. 'Dada. I want to show you something!'

We composed ourselves as best we could. Miss Mann, a woman whose expression I could never read, appeared oblivious and I tried not to think that the child's smile was even more impish than usual.

This small and undiscovered dalliance was enough to disturb my usual equilibrium. Had the artist or his new art turned my head? I saw myself in a new light, as the kind of teasing girl I had never meant to be. London friends wrote every day to say how they missed my company and, in the case of the Murrays, I certainly missed them too.

It was time to strengthen old ties. If there was any real strength in the new ones, they could bear the test of a brief separation.

DEVELOPING & FIXING

CHAPTER SIX

The Absence of George

Elizabeth Kemp, March 1844

Thursday

There's somebody at my door. He wears a tall hat and his eyes are grave. His name is McRae and he says he's a Criminal Officer, something I was beginning to figure out for myself. His presence is a wrinkle in the softness of a bonny day and I could do without it.

'Has a crime been committed? One that concerns me or my family?'

My abruptness takes him by surprise and he clears his throat. 'Not that we know of, Mrs Kemp, but your brother called at my office this morning to report your husband's disappearance.'

George is not here and hasn't been since yesterday. A different thing from disappearance. I don't feel the emptiness around me that 'disappeared' would bring.

The officer wants to know when I last saw George.

'He came home yesterday at dinner time and ate a plate of boiled tongue with cabbage and potatoes. He said he would be late home as he was calling at the builder.'

McRae gets out his notebook. 'That would be the builder whose yard is the other side of Lochrin Basin?'

'His name is Lind. George, as you know, is the architect of

the new Monument. Lind is the building contractor.'

The officer records these names and places painstakingly, as if the harder he presses on his pencil, the better they will conjure up my husband. I feel the need to give him more words to press.

'Before he left, George spoke to the bairns and kissed me as he always does, quickly on the forehead. At the front door, he picked up his coat but left his hat behind.'

McRae asks if this is a common occurrence. I don't know what he means: the brevity of the kiss, the leaving of the hat?

'George's work possesses him, body and soul, whether it's a simple joint or a cathedral spire. He is sometimes off-hand with his farewells. But I'm in no doubt he cares for me, and for the bairns.'

The officer only wants to know if George is in the habit of calling at Lind's. I say that he goes there most afternoons to inspect the deliveries of stone.

The words flow from me but my mind sticks on the character of George. I never complain at his eagerness to work. His fervour is what makes him George Kemp. And his dreams are my dreams. On the day, two years since, when the men of the city gathered to confer the prize for designing the Monument, I asked to go in, to plead George's case myself. I was made to wait outside the meeting room, peering over the window sill, my heart beating faster than that of the bairn in my arms.

The officer is still on my doorstep, waiting for something I don't know I can give.

'That's the last I saw of him, at dinner time. He had a piece with him for later, tongue with mustard. I put the bairns to bed at six. It was wearisome without him, but the fire was still lit. I sat a wee while with a book. It was only when I put out the lamp and stood by the window that I saw fog rolling over the links.'

'You must have been worried by then,' says McRae.

I don't recall that I was. George might have stayed late with

Lind or met friends on his way home and become engrossed in some discussion. Although he wasn't back, I didn't miss him. His presence was here in the house, his slippers at the fireside and his hat on the back of the door.

McRae needs to feel this presence of George for himself and so I ask him in. In our parlour, shaded from the sun, I see how he occupies a space that has become empty.

'The fog was a surprise,' I tell him. 'George walks every day from here to Princes Street then to Lind's and home again. Sometimes more than once. He says his boots would walk by themselves if he weren't in them. On any day, he can tell me where the path will be muddy and places where he will put a step in, just in case footpads are lurking.'

McRae's pencil is poised over his notebook.

'Yes, that worried me over the winter when it was dark by four o'clock. Now the days are drawing out and he carries a stick given to him by my brother, a very stout stick cut from a hawthorn in Glencoe. When he saw it, George laughed and said he could give somebody a right good clout with it if he needed to.'

McRae frowns. 'Would it be in his nature to give a body a clout?'

I tell myself it's his job to think this way yet it still affronts me when everybody knows what a mild-tempered man George is.

'No, Officer, he was not in the way of fighting and would only ever have struck if he feared for his life. I can picture him last Sunday, using the stick to point at a bank of nettles along the Dean Path, telling the bairns that some of them would sting but other would grow flowers, and that we must think the best of plants as well of people, because they may come good in ways we don't expect.'

The officer's eye is drawn to the picture on the mantelpiece and he goes to look at it more closely, unfamiliar with how it was made.

I pick it up in its frame and hand it to him. 'This is a

calotype, made by Mr Hill and Mr Adamson. George is very taken with it. I think the sun is too bright in his face. The smile is his, I grant you. It could be nobody other than George.'

McRae examines it, as if it contains the essence of George, which I suppose it does.

'Of course you haven't met my husband. When he gets back from wherever he is you'll see the likeness.'

Am I taking too much of the officer's time? I've had no company since yesterday, unless you count the bairns and the maid, and I feel the unspoken words come rushing from me like a burn when a damn of stones is breached.

'On Sunday, he used the stick to fish Lizzie's bonnet from the water. He showed her how his hat is always attached by a cord to his collar so it will never blow off and end up in a burn, or under a carriage, or in the Lochrin Basin which he passes so often.'

In the calotype, George is bareheaded. 'And did he have his hat and his stick yesterday, Mrs Kemp?'

'The stick, yes, but not the hat because you'll see it's still hanging at the front door. He would never have gone far without it and must only have left it because of the weather being mild. I let the girls run in the garden without their shawls and the boys without their jackets.'

McRae hands the picture to me. He must get back to the business in hand. 'Mrs Kemp, even with the stick to support him, it would have been treacherous in last night's fog. Do you think Mr Kemp might have missed his footing while walking along the canal?'

I have seen this coming and my answer is ready. 'George? No. He's a dreamer, yes, but not a gowk. His nature is practical and noticing. He loves to walk in the hills and show the bairns the creeping things that lie under stones and knows where to look for the nest of any bird. I remember him when we were courting, crouching on the edge of a loch, stirring the eddies with a stick to see what might swim out and surprise us. He never once slipped towards the water. He never once missed his footing.'

It seems we have come to the end of his questions. McRae has other things to do than talk to the wife of a man who has only gone off on some business of his own or called on a friend when he saw the fog coming in. I am suddenly loath to let him go and be left with the thought that George has disappeared.

McRae turns his hat in his hands. 'Mrs Kemp, we have men whose job it is to check no animals or refuse have been thrown in the canal. I'll ask them to take a look,' he says, 'just as a precaution.'

I'm not afraid to look the officer in the eye and thank him. He bids me goodbye and I close the door. In the parlour I replace the picture on the mantelpiece. Above it hangs the inscription George found in Melrose Abbey and took a fancy to.

Keep in mind the end, your salvation.

George thinks this motto brings him luck. They are not, it seems to me, the words of a dreamer who would miss his footing along the canal.

Later my brother calls and I ask him why he went to McRae. He says he himself has gone as far as Pennicuik calling on all of George's friends and heard no word. 'McRae is a famous solver of mysteries. We need his help.'

We are sitting either side of the fire. William fills up the gap where George should be.

'Do you think George has enemies, Elizabeth?' He shifts his legs and answers his own question. 'A lot of folk begrudged him the prize.'

'He knew that would be the way of it but the Monument is his now. Nobody can take it away from him, enemy or friend.' I will not say what's in my head, *whatever has befallen him.*

If George is gone another night it's what we must think. That something has befallen him.

It's dark, though without last night's fog. William will get home safe so why would it be otherwise for George? He is in some kind of limbo between being absent and having disappeared. His hat in the hall is my talisman, as the Melrose inscription is his.

Friday
A terrible hunger has taken hold of me – for an ending to it, any ending.

When I hear the Officer's voice at the door, fear comes between me and the hunger and keeps me frozen to the spot. I hang back in the parlour where the maid shows him in. He apologises for disturbing me. I search the man's face but find nothing to read in it.

'We have looked along the canal and in the Lochrin Basin and found no trace of your husband.'

Hope beats its wings. 'I didn't think you would.'

McRae has been in my parlour more times than my husband in the last two days and I feel less well disposed to him. The man's job is rounding up criminals and no crime has been found.

'So the matter is closed?'

McRae looks puzzled. 'Your husband's disappearance is still . . . unexplained.'

Edinburgh, its gentry and its Criminal Officer would like it explained. This isn't any poor soul from Leith or a High Street close who's gone unaccountably missing. It's George Kemp, the architect of gothic splendour, the misfit who became the city's darling. He is my darling too. I only want the puzzle solved if the answer's the right one, that George went off for some reason of his own, or was struck on the head just hard enough for him to lose his bearings but not so hard he won't come to and find his way home in the end.

McRae has something else to say. 'Maybe your husband likes a jug of ale or a dram of whisky? If he does there's no shame in it but drink can make the most sure-footed man take a tumble.'

He still hopes the canal contains the answer to his mystery. I refuse to give in to him.

'If you mean does George ever come home the worse for wear, I can tell you he has neither the time nor the inclination for drink.'

McRae says he'll keep looking and I thank him but only because he expects it. I think he would be better searching for the nameless souls whom no one will miss and who still deserve a Christian burial.

Saturday
This is the longest day so far. The bairns are squabbling. William, the youngest, wants Lizzie to make a cord for his hat as she has done for her own so it will never blow off. I can't abide their quarrelling. I keep telling them they do not need hats because even their father left his behind.

William, the youngest, tugs at my sleeve. 'Where has faither gone?' he asks.

I have nothing but the calotype to show him. In it, George leans on a marble slab with loose stones piled behind him. 'Look, he is busy with his building like he always is.'

'But he missed his tea and his breakfast.'

'Everybody kens your faither. Somebody will have given him his tea.'

'So will he be home the night?'

I have to tell a story, not to them, but to myself. 'If not he'll be with Mr Hill and Mr Adamson. They are only on Calton Hill and they always welcome callers.'

Lizzie, the eldest, is listening. 'Well why don't we go to Calton Hill and tell faither to come home?'

She challenges me as I have challenged MacRae. I haven't the heart to go on with my story.

McRae hasn't called. I should be pleased but I feel his absence in the parlour where I've grown accustomed to him shifting from one leg to the other and holding his hat before him.

Instead of the officer I get my sister-in-law who calls to take the bairns for a walk. 'To give you some peace.'

While they're getting their coats on she says that my brother has been to the infirmary and the poor-house. There was no sign of George. A chill comes over me, as if to think of him amongst the poor and the sick is enough to put him there.

I watch them leave. 'Don't go near the water,' I call after them and a body passing on the other side of the street turns to look at me. I've become the wife whose man has disappeared. I should be more careful with my thoughts or they will become other folks' too and who knows where it will end?

When my sister-in-law gets back she says how queer it is that we had only that one night of fog and how George should have been out in it and how he was always a dreamer.

A flame of anger travels from my feet through my belly to my tongue. 'He is not a dreamer!'

She starts back, then tries to take my arm before I snatch it away. 'I only thought you must reconcile yourself,' she says.

'To what?'

She cannot put a word to it and only shakes her head. She has noticed on the walk that Lizzie's hat is attached to her collar as George's always is.

'She copies her father,' I say. 'They all do.'

My sister-in-law is ready to go. She leaves me with this. 'I always said this city has too much water.'

Monday

You might say that one length of hawthorn is much like another but I would recognise the stick McRae is holding anywhere. He does not speak so I hold out my hand for it. Though the bark is dry there is a weight in it, a weight of water. If I take it in two hands and test its strength, it will bend as it never would have bent before.

76

I give it back to him and wonder if he will dare to tell me. But McRae is a brave man. 'In Lochrin Basin,' he says, 'not far from Lind's yard.'

My heart stops and with it my breathing. My knees are folding beneath me as the sodden stick would fold if I put my weight on it.

McRae has taken my arm. I would like to shake it off as I did my sister's but what use will I be to George if I'm on the ground?

'Mrs Kemp, I'm sorry for your loss,' he says.

I shake my head, denying him. So the stick is found. A stick is just that, no more and no less. Its absence has not concerned me, not like the absence of his feet on the fender or his back next to mine in the bed.

We are on the doorstep. I clutch at the door frame. We step inside so as not to show our feelings to the street.

'Look,' I point at the hook on the back of the door, 'his hat is still here. He always takes his hat. He'll come back for his hat.'

McRae takes the hat from the hook, holding it out to me with a kind of reverence. I wonder at this effrontery, for a visiting Criminal Officer to handle my husband's hat. Then I see that it's not George's hat. It's too small. It's a bairn's hat, made to look like George's by the attachment of a cord.

In a howl of rage I call their names. 'Thomas Kemp! Lizzie Kemp! William George Kemp!'

They come running.

'*Whose is this hat*?'

Thomas steps forward. He is the apple of his father's eye and shows every sign of having his talent. 'Lizzie helped me make it like faither's.'

My own children have deceived me. The anger flares and I raise my arm to my bairn. McRae, whom I have all but forgotten, catches hold of me before I can do any harm. I am still shouting, louder than any fishwife, louder than any minister who calls down fire and brimstone. '*Why did you leave it here?*'

Thomas gulps in fear and cowers from this mother who has became a lioness. 'It's been there since Sunday. You said it was too warm.'

The tears are pouring now and my nose is running so I have to wipe it on my sleeve as the bairns are forbidden to do.

'Please, Mrs Kemp. You need to sit down.'

I am as limp as a collar that has lost its starch. When the tears abate, he calls the maid to take the bairns away.

I thank him for his patience and for telling the truth to one who didn't want to hear it.

He shakes his head. 'I thought it would be too painful to bring the hat.'

The hat was found with the stick in Lochrin Basin, attached to the collar of a coat, on the body of a man who might once have borne a resemblance to the picture on my mantelpiece.

My breathing is still unsteady but I'm calmer than I was. I must cling to this calmness for I don't know how long it will last. I think it's bound up in the presence of Officer McRae.

'You have a hard job to do, bringing such news.'

'Not as hard as the job of the one who receives it.'

I ask if I can see George and he says I may, but the warning in his eyes tells me that I would be better remembering George as he was.

'Your brother has been informed,' he says. 'He can make the identification.'

There is nothing for it but to bid Officer McRae farewell. I must let him go about his business of keeping the peace, of solving more troublesome mysteries than the man whose mind was on his work, a dreamer of dreams, who should have taken better care as he walked in the fog by Lochrin Basin.

CHAPTER SEVEN

The Morning After

June 1844

D.O. Hill did not rue sitting down with Geordie Bell and James Ballantyne. Nor did he rue the Edinburgh Ale brought out to lighten the mood: after a week of being at everybody's beck and call, why shouldn't he spend an hour or two in the company of old friends? But one thing had led to another. When a serious argument broke down in laughter, somebody called for a song. With the light holding, they'd spilled out into the courtyard and pressed Robert into taking pictures, probably wasting a deal of the best paper that should have been kept for folk who would pay.

At the gloaming, the camera had been put away, if not the ale. Now he'd woken in a bed that wasn't his own with a thumping head and a mouth as dry as an empty ditch. He was lying in the cold and dark in a bedroom that faced the hill. He groped for his pocket watch, opened one reluctant eye then groaned. It was already past eight o'clock.

He sat up and rubbed his hands across his face to dispel the weariness pinning him to the bed. If his wits didn't fail him entirely, it was Saturday. He needn't be at his desk in the Academy until next week but that still left a hundred things to see to between now and then, not least collecting Chattie from his sister's house where she had spent all of yesterday. He had sent a note asking them to keep her overnight.

He used the pot, splashed his face, and sat back down on the edge of the bed. The thickness of his head added to the weight of expectation pressing on his shoulders like a sack of coal. There was his duty to the Royal Scottish Academy and its members, to the Kirk and all its ministers, and now the expectations of Robert Adamson and his queue of sitters waiting to be calotyped. Against all these, his duty to the bairn he barely saw from one week to the next.

He dragged his hose over uncooperative legs, pulled on his shoes and stood before the mirror. Even in this meagre light it revealed the pallor in his cheeks and a baleful redness in his eyes.

Behind him a shadow moved. He held his breath. There was a presence at his shoulder. Ann, here of all places, in a house where she had never set foot. Queer, when she had never put in an appearance at home, though her piano was still there and all her ornaments, as well as those who had loved her so dearly.

He could have blinked to rid himself of the ghost. Ann was safely with God and this was an illusion brought on by drink and self-pity. But even an illusion might bring comfort. 'Och, Ann,' he said to the mirror. 'How did it come to this?'

He imagined her low laugh. 'You have the gift of helping folk, so you want to help them all.'

And that would never work. But what could he put aside? He had a salary from the Academy. The Disruption Painting had been his idea and he couldn't lay that burden down. Joining Robert and using calotypes should have saved him time but he had let it distract him from his original purpose. Maybe he should have stopped with the portraits of ministers, but by then he had found out how much more the camera could do and how much he enjoyed putting it at other folk's disposal.

It was the camera and its possibilities that had led to last night's argument with Geordie Bell, who had arrived to find Hill in the workshop with Robert and Jessie Mann. Bell peered at a negative of Greyfriars Kirkyard, newly out of the developing tray, and shook his head. 'This is all very well, but what good will it do?'

Robert had moved on to the next negative, the same view from a different angle. 'We're making pictures and we're still learning.' He looked up and caught Hill's eye. 'Do we have to do good as well?'

Geordie, a doctor and a Poor Law Commissioner had come from his rounds in the Canongate and before that from a bairn with croup in the Old Town. He described what he'd seen there, his voice tight with anger. 'Get your camera to the High Street where there are three families to a room, or to the whisky shops where the men spill out at ten o'clock in the morning, already fu'.'

Hill motioned to Robert to pay no attention. He took Bell by the arm and led him back into the house. 'Folk have seen and smelled the Old Town for themselves. They don't need a picture to ken what it's like.'

Geordie shook him off. 'They forget too easily. They pretend it's no there. You can use your calotypes to remind them of what they don't want to think about.'

Hill could see the force of it: maybe pictures, real pictures, of the destitution of the Old Town would carry more weight than words or a cartoonist's sketch. But Robert's health was poor. Expeditions down the closes would do him no good and a call on Robert's time was a call on his own.

Hill shook his head. 'I'm a painter. I make things to hang on parlour walls. You want me and Robert to go up there and celebrate dirt and debauchery?'

Geordie would not give in. 'This is your chance to do good. Don't waste it.'

James Ballantyne's arrival brought respite from Geordie's

tirade. A jug of ale and the high jinks that followed set the seal on an uneasy peace.

Ann's ghost, if that's what it was, had been chased away by the morning light. A chance to do good, Geordie had said. But there were limits to the help he could give. For all the uproar the calotypes had caused, for all the pleasure he took from them, the chemistry was capricious and he saw little money coming in. If any of his duties could be laid aside, surely it was this one.

He cocked an ear to the noises of the house. There was a rattle of a poker in the range but no voices drifted up the staircase. On his way downstairs, a knock came at the door. Expecting a hawker or an errand boy, he opened it to find John Adamson, Robert's brother, on the doorstep. In the early days John had often been here, helping Robert with the calotypes and keeping an eye on his health, but Hill hadn't seen him in months.

'Come in, man, come in! You're a sight for sore eyes. What time did you get up to be here so early?'

John smiled and shook his hand. 'I came from St Andrews yesterday and stayed the night in Musselburgh.' In the lobby he took off his hat with a glance at Hill's appearance. 'Just as well, as I guess you had my bed.'

Hill, more aware than ever of his unkempt state, ushered him in, drawing his hand through his tousled hair. It didn't help that no maid had seen to the parlour since the night before. The drinking flutes on the table and the enduring reek of stale beer told their own story. He held up his hands, admitting his part in the crime. 'We were sociable last night. You'll be pleased to know Rob was the most sober of us. I'm guessing he's already out the back, at his negatives.'

John sat down at the un-wiped table and his calm benevolence settled over the room. With the thought of giving up the calotypes fresh in his mind, here was the ideal moment to give it an airing, to see how John would react before broaching it with Robert. All the same, as motes flew above the unwashed glasses, Hill was reluctant to get to the point. He knew John relied on his being here.

Adamson was the first to break the lengthening silence. He nodded to the table. 'So who was your company? Anybody I know?'

John had written papers on sanitary reform in St Andrews. It was a relief to put the more pressing matter to one side. 'George Bell says we should take the camera to the closes and the drinking dens. Use them to force the council to improve things over there. Do you think it would work?'

John never rushed an answer. He folded his arms. 'It's a fair point. But what makes Bell think folk are ignorant of the poverty? They just look the other way.'

At this vindication Hill struck the table with more force than he meant to so that the glasses wobbled and John reached out to steady them. 'That's what I told him. I support the reformers but this isn't what they need, and I can't put myself at their beck and call.'

John leaned over the table. 'I can see Bell's point of view. You've supported Chalmers and the Kirk. You know the power of the calotype better than anybody.'

John's argument had swung against him. Hill shook his head to rid himself of despair, not just at the state of the town but at his own inadequacy. The morning was wearing on and he was still on Calton Stairs when he should be at home with his bairn.

'There's something else.'

John Adamson tipped his head back and closed his eyes, as if to say, *Go on, I'm listening*. His stillness was a balm to Hill's troubled soul but nothing had changed. He had to speak. 'I have been thinking it's time for me to give this business up.'

Nothing changed in the room. If anything John Adamson grew only more still. Hill watched him raise the lid of one hooded eye, challenging him to spell it out.

'I have sunk too much time . . . and money . . . into calotyping.'

John uncrossed his legs and crossed them again in the other direction. There wasn't a drop of rancour in his voice. 'You've had enough?'

John's neutrality was harder to bear than his criticism. Hill sighed and spread his hands in front of him, studying the half moons of his nails. He knew that he was bewitched by the calotypes. The play of light and shade, the subtlety of the detail, the softness of the finish never failed to rouse his artistic passion. He would never have enough.

'I've been a willing captive to your science and I believe I've made an art of it. I would do more if I could. But a painter isna'e paid until he finishes his work. The longer I spend here, the less I paint, and the less time I give to my ain folk.'

John opened both eyes. 'And the more you give to Robert.'

Hill heaved a sigh. Robert might not be family but he was as fond of him as any brother. To give more time to Chattie meant leaving a friend, one who could do with his help, one he enjoyed helping.

'Have you said this to Rob?' John asked.

Hill shook his head. 'You caught me on my way to speak to him. But maybe I'll leave it. He has enough to do the day.'

John pushed himself to his feet. 'We have no hold on you, not now the ministers are done but I don't need to tell you, you'll be sorely missed.'

Hill's mouth was still as dry as a sandstone wall. He was surprised at the speed of John's acceptance but it was a relief not to prolong the conversation. He rose to go. 'Well I'm away home.'

He hesitated as he shrugged on the coat he had laid over the arm of the chair. It felt wrong to be leaving in the middle of the day. 'The appointment book for this afternoon is full. Should I knock on Jessie's door as I pass?'

John shook his head. 'Leave Jessie to herself for once. I can help Rob the day.'

At the front door Hill stopped again, reluctant to take the step that marked a parting of the ways. 'I'll come back on Monday. I would rather tell Rob myself.'

John shook his hand. 'Rob will understand. Now go and see your bairn.'

Despite John's insistence he shouldn't disturb Jessie, Hill walked down to Leopold Place. The air was fresh but there was no wind. The ache in his neck began to ease under his crumpled shirt. This was the quieter side of the hill and, as his boots struck the bright new cobbles, he smiled to himself for the first time that day. It must be a year since Jessie had turned up at Rock House, offering her services to Robert. What a surprise that had been, his old friend from Perth living round the corner from his new partner. Jessie had always been good company. By the time Hill was party to their friendship, Rob had already shown her how to prepare the paper and set it in the frame. She had proved to be a quick learner, her mind more agile than his in comprehending the ins and outs of developing. With her steady hand and willingness to work, she'd been a godsend. If he was taking his leave (he reminded himself that he was), she had the skill to be more than an assistant. She had the appetite for making calotypes, he was sure, but it was only fair to let her know his plans.

Before he mounted the stairs to the flat, he hesitated. He had seen how Jessie watched Rob as he worked, and not just to learn from him. When Rob was tired or starting to cough, it was Jessie who nagged him to have a rest, telling him not everything had to be done this minute. If Hill asked her to spend more time at Rock House she could hardly say no. But that didn't make it right. Asking for her help served only to salve his conscience. Time enough for them all to sit down on Monday, himself, Jessie and Rob, and work out what should be done.

At his sister's house, Mary was at her writing desk and barely looked up to greet him.

'Chattie's had a dose of the sniffles. I was just going to send for you to come and take her home. Wherever home is these days.'

He winced at this barb. 'I'm sorry. You know how grateful I am. I meant to be back last night.'

Mary blotted a line in her ledger and let out a breath. 'No. I'm the one who should apologise. She's no trouble. I shouldn't have said anything.'

Hill walked around the desk and put his hand on her shoulder. 'No. You've done enough. You have your own bairns to look after. I've told John Adamson they'll have to do without me.'

She sat back from the desk. 'A break will do you good. We'll have the wee one again next week.'

'I mean to stop calotyping altogether.'

She laid down pen and blotter and gave him a quizzical look. 'I have my ministers to paint. I can't do everything.'

Mary shook her head. 'I can see how much pleasure it gives you. And how much good company.' She laid her hand on his arm. 'You've had little enough of either since Ann died.'

She was right. Robert and the calotype *had* given him a new interest, something to show a world that might weary one day of engravings and artists' illustrations. As for the company, he took pleasure in all of it, the artists and writers, the visiting dignitaries, the men and the women. Since Ann's death, he had learned it was best not to leave too much time for pondering the sadness of life. Giving up calotypes and all they entailed might leave time and space for melancholy to creep under his door. He shook himself as he left the room. His life was a full and happy one.

Chattie was playing peevers with her cousins and showed no sign of fever. As she hopped, skipped and stumbled in her efforts to nudge the stone across the line, her hair flew up around her ears. He thought of his favourite air, *Ho-ro My Nutbrown Maiden*, and of Ann accompanying him as he sang. He put up a prayer that she could see her daughter now.

Mary came out to join them. 'Now that I think of it,' she said, 'the sneezing might have been caused by the long grass on the King's Meadow where the bairns were playing yesterday. The dandelions were out and the air was full of seeds.'

So the sniffles were a false alarm. Even so, if he'd been here instead of imbibing Edinburgh Ale, nobody would have worried.

'Come away,' he said to Chattie. 'It's time for you and me to take ourselves home.'

Her wee face fell. 'I want to play another game.'

She was used to his absences. Something else that needed to change.

'What you need,' he told her, 'is a good dose of sea-air. And so do I. This afternoon we'll take a walk along the beach.'

Chattie was a good wee walker and didn't complain until they were in sight of the harbour wall at Newhaven, where he hoisted her over onto the beach so that they could crunch along the shingle and throw chuckies into the water, seeing who could make the biggest splash. Laddies from the fishing village, their faither's breeks flapping around their skinny legs, clambered over a boat drawn up on the shingle. Chattie watched them from a distance as they scuffled on the upturned keel over who would be king of the castle, until one of them claimed his position and refused to be dislodged. From this vantage point he stood up, and still struggling for his balance, managed to doff his floppy cap and make a sweeping bow towards them.

Hill laughed and returned his gesture.

'Who's that, Dada?'

'Nobody we know, but he's a gallus wee thing all right.'

He brushed down her shoes and they crossed to the other side of the fish-market square. The walk back would be quicker. They wouldn't be distracted by the delights of the beach and the shouts of the boys who'd made it their territory for the day.

The fishermen's houses, two storeys connected by an outside

stair, made a tidy edge around the cobbles. He told Chattie how folk lived in the top rooms, the ground floor filled with nets and tackle and sometimes fish. On one of the stairs, several women were talking quietly amongst themselves. He envied them this simple recreation. He had many friends but little time for the simple ease of companionship, and when he did, he spoiled it by taking too much ale. The women were hard workers too. On other days they were up in Edinburgh selling fish while the bairns now tumbling on the strand took lessons in the grey stone school.

He raised his hat to the group as he passed. Only one of them, a brown-eyed woman with fine features, glanced round at him and the bairn.

'Is that woman gallus too?' Chattie asked.

'No, she is not, Chattie, but she's a lady and we always raise our hats to ladies.'

The conversation of Friday night came back to him. Chalmers was all in favour of celebrating folk who lived decently and with dignity despite a lack of riches. The fisher-folk of Newhaven were just that. This is where the camera could do some good. He must remember to say so to Rob.

Gulls shrieked at them on their way home and Chattie told him a story about a wee brown mouse her cousin had used to make Myrtle, the housekeeper, jump. He laughed with her and took her hand in his. When she whimpered in weariness, he set her on his shoulder for the last half mile, her arms clamped around his neck and her cheek damp on his.

'You will have your Dada home more soon,' he said to her.

Her voice was drowsy. 'Why?'

'Because he'll not be making pictures with Uncle Rob.'

Chattie lifted her head, tugging at his hair. 'Will Uncle Rob not miss you?'

The bairn had a way with her. He shifted her weight on his back.

'No more than I will miss him.'

When he said they would go to Rock House on Monday, Chattie's eyes lit up. 'Who else will be there? Will I have my picture taken? Will Lizzie give me a scone?'

He said he didn't know about the picture, but she could be hopeful of the scone. Her happiness lessened his discomfort at taking her along for reasons of his own. Without her, he was afraid that his resolution would desert him.

At least there was no queue of sitters and they found Robert and Jessie out the back. The weather was fine enough for printing and Jessie was setting up the frames in a spot that would get the best of the sun.

Chattie ran to her and Jessie, who was fond of the bairn, stood back from her work to take her hand. 'Mind, now! We don't want to knock over the picture and spoil it.'

Robert emerged from the workshop, wiping his hands on a rag. 'We wondered where you had got to,' Rob said.

Was it Hill's imagination or did Robert avoid his eye? 'Can you come in for a minute? I have things to tell you.'

Chattie was making a game of hiding in the laurels that edged the path around the house. 'You two go on in,' Jessie said. 'I'll look after her.'

The parlour had been cleaned and tidied. No trace of ale had survived Lizzie's exertions with the polish. For all his determination, Hill needed to offer some topic other than his imminent desertion. 'It was fine to see John,' he said, which set Robert off on how John was perfecting a new way of fixing the calotypes. Hill let him run on until Rob stopped in mid-flow. They were facing each other across the room. Rob was in front of the window with the light behind him and although his face was in shade, Hill had never seen him look so out of sorts.

'What's this I hear about you leaving us?' Rob said,

Hill looked beyond him to the view of Arthur's seat, wishing for an hour to clamber up its stony flank. 'You can see how I'm fixed. I'm pulled in too many directions.'

Rob shook his head in exasperation. 'But how will we manage without you?'

He would have said more but Hill cut him off. 'You and Jessie will be fine. Or you might find somebody else to help. I see more folk now about the place with cameras.'

Rob did no more than raise an eyebrow but he stopped his pacing and sat down at the table where Hill took the seat alongside him. 'Never mind me and my troubles. Let me tell you something else,' he said. 'On Saturday I took Chattie to Newhaven. Have you ever been?'

Robert shook his head.

'This is the place George Bell should use for his pictures. ' He rested his hands on his knees. 'The folk there are upright and god-fearing and above all . . . dignified. You should see some of the women. They're more than bonny, and the bairns well looked after.'

Rob would not be drawn.

'They're the perfect example of how a lack of wealth doesn't have to mean poverty of spirit.' He paced the floor in his eagerness to distract Rob from his obvious ill temper. 'Jessie,' he looked round, forgetting Jessie was outside, 'will know what I mean. They have their own school, and a minister goes down on Sundays to preach. This is what folk need to see, wholesome lives, not squalor and drunkenness.'

Robert was getting up to go. 'I need to get on.'

'This is where the Poor Law should take its lessons,' Hill said. 'You need to go and have a look. You need to take the camera.'

Robert stopped on his way out and faced Hill, his arms folded. 'I don't think Jessie and me will be going anywhere for a while, never mind visiting the fisher-folk.'

Guilt tugged at Hill. 'I'm sorry. I'm leaving you in the lurch. But you'll get past it.'

Not only guilt, but regret too for what he would have to give up. Over his Sunday breakfast and, if he were honest, during the minister's sermon, he had arranged the Newhaven women in his mind; around their creels, mending their nets, clustered round the minister's dais as they prayed for their men folk. Over a cold dinner at Mary's house he had put his hands on the shoulder of the girl with brown eyes and turned her to look at the camera so that it caught the modesty and strength in her gaze. Could Robert and Jessie get it right?

'Maybe I could come in on the odd day . . .'

Rob threw his hands in the air and laughed, though it rang hollow. 'You see! These pictures you're talking about are your calotypes, not ours. Jessie and I could take fifty and not one would be as persuasive as the one that's in your mind and has come from your artistry.'

Robert was young but he was fly. He had let Hill ramble on about Newhaven and trap himself in his own argument. Jessie could learn to calotype but Hill was the artist. He made the calotypes what they were.

They heard Chattie's voice outside and her footsteps coming past the window. Hill closed his eyes but no answer came to him. Maybe Newhaven would have to be left to its own devices.

Chattie came hurtling in. 'Dada, look what I found!'

Her eyes were glued to her outstretched palm. 'Look! It's a caterpillar and it's all stripey.'

Jessie was breathless in pursuit. 'Slow down now or you'll drop it!'

The men got up to look at the creature as it squirmed in her hand.

'Quick, Uncle Robert, take a picture of it before it goes!'

Rob held out his hand and she eased the creeping thing from her palm to his.

Rob watched it curl itself into a ball. 'Och he's too wee for a picture.'

She sighed in disappointment. 'And I suppose he would never sit still long enough.'

Robert got down on his haunches and transferred the

caterpillar to the back of her hand. 'You're quite right. You'll make a very good calotyper one day, Chattie Hill.'

Jessie, standing behind, put her hand on Chattie's head. 'Take him outside to the garden. He's looking for his dinner and he won't find any here.'

Chattie stood still, wanting to own her beastie a wee while longer. Robert and Jessie lingered too, reluctant to spoil the moment. Hill watched them form a perfect group, Chattie at its centre, Robert kneeling, Jessie at its apex. They could have been a family. He ached to find the camera and capture the timeless beauty of the picture, but it was too fleeting. Chattie ran off to the garden with Jessie behind her. Robert went off to his developing and Hill made no attempt to stop him.

Left alone, he looked out over the city, old and new, a place that had been in most ways good to him. His house in Inverleith would be the envy of many. Why did it please him so little these days? He'd had no visitors there in months, preferring to hang on here at Rock House if he needed diversion. Looking for an answer, his feet took him upstairs to where Ann's spirit had somehow sought him out. Could she help him now? The room was filled with noon-day light. He didn't think so. He sat down on the bed and stroked the bedspread with the flat of his hand, recalling the picture he had just framed in his head; Jessie, Chattie and Robert. Chattie seemed at home here, Jessie and Rob both made a fuss of her. Even Ann had given Rock House her blessing. Maybe there was truth as well as beauty in the calotype he had seen in his mind's eye. Maybe there had been some purpose in his seeing it.

He left the room and went on a more urgent exploration of the house. There was another bedroom, unused, and a basement below the level of the parlour. The place was bigger than he thought and even with Lizzie in the attic, most of it empty.

In the carriage that took him and Chattie back to Inverleith, he said, 'I think you're right about Uncle Robert needing my help. How would it be, do you think, if we stayed at his house, instead of our own?'

'Will the caterpillar still be there?' she said. 'Will we get a picture of it next time?'

She was too young to see beyond the next day.

'Well I think there will be other caterpillars if that one doesn't come back.'

'Will I still go to Auntie Mary's?'

'Yes. You'll still go to your cousins, but Dada will have more time to play with you.'

He forgave himself his stumblings and wrong turnings. When it was time for a change, you couldn't always see what the change should be. Yet here at last was the right solution. With both of them on Calton Hill, John needn't worry about Robert being left alone. Hill would have time to give himself to this thing of light and shade he had come to love. He could go to Newhaven and to many places besides.

Would Ann approve? Was he wrong to think he could divide himself so many ways? As he unlocked his own front door and called to the maid, he felt the empty silence of the stairwell. Rock House had its gloomy corners, but he had already found friendship there and laughter. With Chattie by his side, who knew what else might lie in store?

CHAPTER EIGHT

Silver Harvest

Elizabeth Hall, Newhaven, 1845

It's Sunday, and while the other women are readying bairns for the kirk, I am drawn to the shore. On my way across the market square, a fractured sun reveals the scattering of fish-scales in the cobbles, bright as new bawbees.

Beyond the harbour wall, tough grass gives way to the narrow beach of broken shells and rough-grained sand. I look up the estuary to the open sea but there will be no boats home the day. The crews will lay up at anchor, praying for a good catch and a safe return. In summer, they head as far north as they can, working as long as there is light, anchoring off places I have never seen: Stonehaven, Peterhead, Buckie. Willie and his men see little of the shore, their eyes straining for alterations in the breeze, the light, the colour of the sea.

A gannet with a scrawny neck bobs and dives as the waves creep up the shingle and nibble at the turf. The tide at least is predictable, unlike the weather, the herring or the money coming in.

The church bell calls me back. I take my place in the pew and give thanks for what we have: a house for every family, a school, a harvest from the sea that rarely fails. Compared to the poor of the old town, we are rich, except in the company of men.

After the kirk, I take a chair to the foot of our outside stairs. Other women have the same thought and soon the street is set off by gatherings of white-capped girls in their plaid skirts, sewing or checking nets. Jeanie Wilson waves from her door and comes to sit by me.

'Susan's no coming out?'

'She says the sun will give her a headache.' Susan is my mother-in-law. Jeanie and I exchange a look that says her headache is a gift to us. 'You're on your own?'

Jeanie's bairns will be on the shore, skimming stones and plowtering in the boats laid up for repair. Bairns slip from Jeanie as easily as herring from a creel. I try not to envy her. No matter how often Willie plants his seed, my womb fails to quicken.

Jeanie looks up. 'We have a visitor.'

Townsfolk are fond of taking the air down here on a Sunday and our village is well known for its steadfast ways and the good order of our homes. The man who's approaching might be a councillor, or a writer, keen to put down in some magazine what he thinks is the secret of our sobriety and to ask why others can't follow our example. I could tell any of them that cleaning fish and carrying them two miles up to Edinburgh leaves little time or energy for loose living.

Jeanie gets up. 'I'd better get back.'

As she leaves, the stranger lifts his hat to her. He has a worldly air but not a haughty one. I concentrate on the sailcloth I'm inspecting. Let him speak first if he must. After a minute he is still there, no closer, no farther off, as if there is something particular about the space between us.

As I look up, he is forced to come forward. 'I'm sorry to have disturbed you.'

Although the sun is over his shoulder I can see a wide forehead and a strong nose. He is in his middle years.

'We are often disturbed of a Sunday.'

'Would you rather I left you in peace?'

He has already taken a good look at me. This stops me from sending him away. 'Did you want to ask me something?'

He hesitates then holds out his hand. 'David Octavius Hill.'

His fingers are warm on mine. 'How do you do? I am Elizabeth Johnson Hall.'

Like the other women, I've kept my father's name as well as my husband's. Do I catch a twinkle in his eye that my two names put us on an equal footing?

'I'm an artist,' he says.

I've seen painters down at the harbour, wiping their brushes on their fancy aprons, marvelling at the peace and beauty of the scene. They rarely come in the week when the herring guts cover the cobbles and our hands bleed from taking out the hooks.

'I'm planning a series of studies of the Newhaven folk. I wonder if you would sit for a portrait?'

My hands ache to straighten my cap and feel for any hair coming loose. I make myself stay still and keep my eyes on my needle as it comes to the end of its stitching.

He lifts his coat tails and sits on the bottom step. Since I am on the straight-backed chair this puts him at my feet. Glancing back at the way he has come, past the other women on their steps, I wonder if I am the first he has asked.

Mr Hill draws a sheet of paper from his pocket and shows me the picture of a man who might have looked in a glass and had the colour sucked from his cheeks, leaving no more than a shadow on the paper. I don't know what to make of it. The man has the look of a wounded bulldog.

There's disappointment in his voice. 'Don't you think it's a good likeness?'

I hand back the picture of the man. I've never met him but in some odd way I know him already.

'How is it made?'

'By the light of the sun.'

The answer doesn't satisfy me. If it's such an easy thing, these pictures would be everywhere. 'What else does it need?'

He frowns as if the answer has slipped to the back of his mind. 'Silver,' he says. 'The light reacts with silver salts.'

The picture is a mottled brown with no trace of silver in it but the likeness, I agree, is very good.

When Willie comes home he speaks with the minister. Mr Renfrew knows all about Mr Hill who is trying out some new kind of picture machine. Willie says Mr Renfrew has come down in favour of Newhaven – and me – being on show to the rest of the world.

'What about you?' I ask Willie. 'Do you mind?'

I catch him looking at me across the table, flattered that he and the artist have made the same choice. 'You are the best of them, Lizzie. You always were. Besides, these pictures are only a minute or two in the making.'

I thought it would have taken longer, more than one sitting in front of the artist. I hide my disappointment by getting up to clean the range.

Susan makes no comment on the artist or his pictures. This morning she asked me if Willie and I were still trying for a bairn. I didn't answer. The walls are good and thick and what we do under the blanket is our business.

Mr Hill comes again on a weekday afternoon when the fish have been cleaned and we're back from selling them in the town. He has a younger man with him who is always looking at the sky. Together they push a cart with a wobbling load of stands and boxes.

The artist greets me and sits me in a good padded chair lifted down from the cart then walks around me at a distance, something like the way he did that first day. The younger man is setting up the apparatus on its three-legged stand. A box with a glass eye.

'Have you come from the town?' I ask him.

He nods. 'From Calton Hill. We brought a coach as far as the Links.'

Where he has placed the chair, I am squinting into the sun. Mr Hill comes closer. 'Excuse me,' he says and tilts my chin away from the light. I can smell the hot felt of his suit and something of lemons in his hair. 'Keep your eyes cast down,' he says. 'We can afford a shadow or two. Try to stay as still as you can.'

News has travelled up the street and a small crowd gathers to see the men and their picture machine. Jeanie is there with her three bairns, all blue-eyed with auburn hair like hers. I think about how she will live on in them.

Just as I think I am turned to stone, the young man makes a flourish and says, 'We're done!'

Mr Hill gives me his hand to raise me from my seat and the crowd claps, even though there is nothing to see.

That night my time comes as it does every month. In the morning I put the rags on the fire before Susan can see them.

Mr Hill does not come back and nothing more is heard of him or the pictures he made. Yet I can't put it out of my mind and a week or two later I find myself on Leith Walk in my Sunday clothes. I tell myself it's as good a day as any for a wander up Calton Hill.

At Rock House, where the men have their business, no one answers the front door. Walking further on, I find a side gate and through the laurels I can see a single-storey outhouse at the back. As the gate opens, I hear voices. Two men in a friendly but heated dispute.

'The foreground is too dark. Let me expose it more.'

'No, no, there can be no light without shade.'

Embarrassment sweeps over me. Who am I to come here alone, asking about things I don't understand? But before I can turn back, the door of the outhouse opens and he is coming towards me, covering his surprise with a smile and an outstretched hand.

'Mrs Hall. What brings you . . .?'

'I'm sorry. You're busy.'

He invites me in. 'Would you like to see what we made of you?' He turns and calls. 'Robert! We have a visitor!'

Inside, the blinds are drawn and the assistant is flitting about in darkness, one of many shadows in the room. Pinned to the rough wall, unframed and askew, I make out the picture I was shown that first day, with others grouped around it, folk singly or in groups, in fine clothes or strange costumes, a few bairns amongst them.

'There you are!' He is pointing to a high corner where I see a portrait of a woman in a Newhaven cap and dress, a woman with my features.

'What do you think?'

My face, for it must be mine, is not as I've ever seen it, even in a glass, yet in it I glimpse not just the woman I am but the one I might become.

While I gawp at myself, he opens a chest and takes out an armful of pictures which he lays down awkwardly so they slew across the table. They are all of me, the same picture, many times over, in shades of grey, brown or violet, some misty, some sharply drawn.

He lifts out one which is less distinct and holds it up. 'We tried bromide here, and with this one a different wash. It took us a while to get it right.' He nods to the one on the wall. 'But this is the best. We'll copy it exactly.'

My picture will be in an exhibition, he says, and after that in a book, many books. He takes one from the pile and offers it to me. 'For your family.'

I carry my portrait home but keep it hidden until Willie is back. That night I show it to him.

'It's a good likeness,' he says. He lays it on the chest of drawers and closes the bedroom door.

As he takes me in his arms, I see that great swathe of pictures shifting in the gloaming like a shoal of herring.

Something is loosened inside me.

A rising tide.

A silver harvest.

CHAPTER NINE

Pas de Deux

Elizabeth Rigby, Edinburgh, 1846

In the autumn following the publication of my piece on German painting, D.O. Hill and I danced once more into each other's lives. I had returned to the city after one of many absences and my soul drank, as it always did, at the well of Edinburgh's endless variety; its sombreness and gaiety, its massed clouds and sunlit mornings, its gutters filled with uncouth tramps and its elegant crescents from which the shimmer of the Forth could be tantalisingly glimpsed. However much I enjoyed my trips to London, the sight of this rugged skyline was a true homecoming.

I was eager to visit Rock House and had the perfect calling card in the shape of my article from the *Quarterly Review*, proof, if you will, of my loyalty to the calotypists' cause. I didn't wait for an invitation but sent a note to say I would call the following day.

Ushered to wait in the parlour, I paused in front of the window. Of all the places from which this wonderful city may be viewed, to my mind this is one of the finest: the smoky rooftops of the Old Town framed by the Castle Rock and the slopes of Arthur's Seat, while almost beneath one's feet the Calton Cemetery, with its reminder of mortality, makes a darkly atmospheric foreground.

Withdrawing my gaze from the window, I placed my chair at an angle so that the light would fall around my shoulders and took care in the arrangement of my skirts. You see how I constructed the picture that he would see and did my best to ensure it would meet with his favour. Hearing footsteps outside, I half-turned towards the window, a pose I knew would enhance the curve of my neck, at which point I might have stopped to ponder my motives for this conscious artistry if he hadn't come striding in.

'Elizabeth!' He opened his arms in welcome. 'What has taken you so long?'

I paused so that he could take in the view I had so carefully prepared, of the city and of me, before rising to greet him. As he bent over my hand, I could tell from an alteration in his breathing that he had noticed the lavender water sprinkled on my gloves, just as I perceived how thick and soft his hair still fell around his temples.

I composed myself. 'I have brought something for you.'

I carried with me not the magazine itself but the article Mr Lockhart had recently returned to me, a bundle of pages in my own hand. 'Of course you may have seen it already. It was published in the last but one issue.'

He took it from me. As his eyes skimmed through the lines, I was pleased at my decision to bring my own script rather than the printed version, as if I was offering the essence of my thoughts.

Of course the piece did not immediately reveal what might interest him. 'German painting,' he said, 'very astute, I'm sure.' I was disinclined to hurry him and by the third page he said, 'Why don't we take some tea? I'll call Robert. He'll be pleased to see you.'

The younger man looked wan, I thought, but as cheerful as ever as we pulled up our chairs and sat to the table. The light was improving, Adamson said, and they had many ideas for albums of calotypes, some well under way. The one closest to completion was *Fishermen and Women of the Firth of Forth*.

These pictures had already made quite a stir and I had even taken myself down to Newhaven the previous summer to investigate the subjects who, I have to say, were rather more coarse than one would have judged from the fine calotypes they graced.

I said only that I was sure the album would be successful and looked forward to seeing it. But D.O. may have glimpsed some reservation in my tone and gave me a searching look. 'Out with it, Elizabeth. You know we value your opinion.'

I did not want to make too much of it. 'I think they are some of your finest calotypes,' but was egged on by the enquiry in his eyes. 'A fine example of art improving on nature.'

Here he frowned as well he might. 'The camera shows things only as they are,' he said. 'The artistry is in catching the eye of the viewer.'

'But do you think artistry implies artifice?'

My tongue always was hasty but then so is my pen. He turned to Adamson for help. 'What do you say, Robert. Are we guilty of artifice?'

Adamson was never one for a discussion, philosophical or otherwise, but leaned back in his chair with his hands behind his head. 'I don't know if artifice, as you call it, is a bad thing. We're not changing nature but showing it in its best light. If there's a flaw in the paper or in the developing, we have to alter the negative for the sake of the whole effect.'

D.O. laughed. 'Robert always looks to the chemistry,' he said. But as you know, I look to the art. My conscience is clear on what we display to the world.'

At this my own conscience was called to account. Had I not employed artifice of my own in considering my posture? Had I thought to make myself another Newhaven beauty in the angling of my head, in the creating of shadows to woo the camera and its operator? I had to make a concession.

'The art and the artifice,' I said, 'perhaps they are indivisible.'

Abandoning the fisher-folk to whatever fate awaited them, I took my writing from where it had been left on a chair and turned to the final section, the part guaranteed to secure the interest of my two friends.

'While you've been busy on the banks of the Forth, I've been labouring on your behalf.'

D.O. took the pages from me and I was gratified by the diligent silence in which he ingested them. At the bottom of the page, he simply handed the script to Robert and said, 'Read it so that we can hear.'

Adamson looked puzzled but complied, '. . . *we mean the beautiful and wonderful calotype drawings of Mr Hill and Mr Adamson of Edinburgh. So precious in every real artist's sight, not only for their matchless truth of nature but as the most triumphant proof of all of truth in art.*'

He lowered the paper and stopped reading, it was in any case the end of the topic, and gave a wry smile. 'Now I see why you are challenging us on the matter of truth.'

D.O. was looking beyond me over the rooftops, his expression pensive and his voice softer than before, 'Thank you Elizabeth. I'm so please we persuaded you to our way of thinking. And that you should take the trouble to tell folk there can be beauty in the truth of nature.'

I was a little mesmerised by the construction he had put on my words. Did I consider that truth in itself was beauty? Rather than ponder the philosophy, I inclined my head. 'I have done what I can. I don't know that I can do more while you hide yourselves away in this grey town.'

There was my tongue again, giving voice to thoughts that sprang from nowhere. Edinburgh was his home and also mine. I leavened the weight of its greyness with visits elsewhere, but I loved it more than many of its own citizens. Unlike them, however, I knew it was not the only place worthy of a calotype.

The two men were bemused. 'We're hardly hiding,' Adamson

said. 'We were in Linlithgow only last week. And Glasgow not so long ago. And D.O. has far too much to do here to be gallivanting to London.'

Edinburgh to them was all, and why would it not be?

The immediate purpose of my visit over, it was time to be a more malleable guest. We talked of D.O.'s great canvas of Edinburgh seen from the Castle, which he said was nearing completion. I congratulated him on a fitting tribute to his city. I did not enquire after his painting of the martyrs of the Kirk, a task which I believed would never repay the effort entailed in its manufacture but only trammel his soul.

When I took my leave he was graciousness itself. 'Come again,' he said, 'and next time don't leave it so long.'

I picked up my shawl. 'When the winter's over, will you make another calotype of me?'

Perhaps I was inviting flattery, but in this, as in most things, D.O. was not a man to disappoint. 'You know you are our favourite subject,' he said.

Although Matilda was engaged to be married, I was still at liberty to accept invitations on my own behalf and I recall it was a most diverting season with many outings, all in entertaining company. It was as if the more often I took myself away from Edinburgh, the more warmly I was welcomed on my return, a circumstance which presented an odd conundrum. To stay or to go? To love or be loved?

At one of these engagements, I was particularly courted by Mr D, a gentleman of some authority and wealth, who proved very amiable and whose invitation to call on him in his handsome property I accepted gladly. However, his society in the longer term proved disappointing to the point of tedium and when he began to circulate professions of his love for me, I refused further invitations.

When a note from Rock House arrived the following spring it was more welcome than ever. Messrs Hill and Adamson, it said, would be honoured by a visit to their studio so that they could repay their debt of gratitude to me. I was a little disconcerted at this formality and the suggestion of duty, hoping he looked forward to the pleasure of my company as I did his. I put the card on the mantelpiece for Mama to see but did not respond straight away. Our paths still crossed from time to time as happens in the small compass of Edinburgh society but we shared no private conversation until the summer, when I felt ready to take up the invitation to a calotype.

On the day I returned to Rock House, I found D.O. alone in the courtyard, adjusting the drapes and furniture with which he constructed his studio scenery. He greeted me with his usual affability and got back to his drapery. 'Robert is not himself,' he said, 'but he has left everything ready and I will take the picture. He'll come back in a while to see to it.'

For all my admiration of Mr Adamson, to have D.O. to myself was a gift indeed. I felt my shoulders ease under my chemise and a playful freedom of mood came over me. 'So where would you like me?'

He had set a table in front of the camera, next to it an elegant chair and a birdcage. The impression was of an orangery or a terrace.

'A summer picture,' I said, 'though yesterday the wind nearly blew me over.' I saw the laughter in his eyes and I thought to keep it there. 'Even a tall girl can be blown over, you know, especially carrying an umbrella. In fact our height makes us particularly vulnerable to sudden gusts.'

He laughed as I hoped he would. 'I'm pleased you kept your feet on the ground, though you would have made a fine picture, sailing on the wind to Fife.'

I imagined myself floating across the rooftops and out to sea but full-blown laughter is not ladylike and I bit my lip, happy to be the cause of his good humour.

As I settled myself on the chair, D.O. got behind the camera and looked through the lens to see the shape of the picture, then seeming to think better of it, he straightened up and looked at me directly. 'Let's not worry about calotypes just yet. We are due a talk, you and I.'

I did not demur as he pulled up a chair next to mine.

'I hear you made quite an impression at last month's soirée. Do I take it we'll be seeing you on the arm of Mr D?'

I was startled by this, forgetting how quickly a rumour will fly from one end of the New Town to the other. 'He was very engaging and courteous on our first meeting.'

D.O. did not miss a trick. 'And there was a second?'

I had put this fellow from my mind but was keen to scotch some of the mischief he had caused. 'If you hear he's in love with me, don't believe a word of it. I have given him no encouragement.'

I still did not know if his profession was the truth or some kind of barbed riposte to my refusals and, in retelling the situation, I grew uncomfortable.

D.O., always attuned to human feeling, said, 'Has he insulted you?'

I shook my head. 'Not directly, but I suspect I'm only a novelty, the reason for a boast, or even a joke.'

A frown crossed his brow and he reached for my hand, holding my fingers lightly in his. 'I could tell him there is more to you than novelty, Elizabeth. A man must work to claim your affection. You are the cleverest and the best girl of these parts.'

D.O. might flatter but his heart was always sincere. Aware of warmth stealing over my neck and face I let my eyes drop. He, as perspicacious as ever, let go of my hand and turned his compliment into a joke. 'The best girl, and of course the tallest!'

This allowed us both to laugh and reclaim our easy intimacy, though even in this happiest of interludes, I glimpsed the shadow of an ending.

'How is your daughter?' I asked D.O. He and the child now lived here with Mr Adamson. A few servants and regular visits from Miss Mann completed the odd little household.

'As well and as tiring as ever. She spoke of you only yesterday, asking when you would come to see us.'

Rather than have our conversation founder on this too familiar reef, I got up and re-examined the stage he had made for the calotype, noting the various artefacts lying around the makeshift studio, assessing what might add to the effect. 'Are you thinking of some scene from literature?'

His smile was infectious. 'Only one that's still to be written.'

I entered into the game, pretending the very thing I could not have. 'Ah, a love scene, do you think?'

He was rummaging in a box of paraphernalia and emerged holding the statue of a cupid which he polished with the hem of his coat and set on the table. 'Here we are, then, the perfect companion.'

I sat down and prepared myself for melodrama in a pose not so very different to the one I had affected earlier. 'Do I look suitably wistful?'

He rubbed his chin. 'Imagine you are pining for a lost love,' adding with a puckish look, 'though obviously that would not be Mr D.'

His humour dispelled any awkwardness and I consented to the play-acting, welcoming his hand on my shoulder as he arranged a veil over my hair. I knew full well he felt no discomfort at our closeness, and I wondered if it would have progressed if Adamson hadn't chosen that moment to return to take the calotype, coughing into a kerchief, oblivious to anything he might be interrupting.

D.O., however, showed no annoyance, only upbraiding his friend for being out of bed. 'You don't look well. We can put this off until another time.'

'And waste a bonny day? Let's get it done while we have the chance.'

I assumed my previous expression and intensified it for the camera.

'A truly love-struck maiden,' Robert said, from under his cloth.

Before I left, they took me to their outhouse where I was intrigued to watch the chemical magic of the picture emerging from blackness, a mystery which, following my closer reading of Mr Fox Talbot's work, was gradually revealing itself to me.

'A beauty,' D.O said to Adamson. 'Don't you think?'

Adamson was sighing over a blemish in the top corner of the negative which was impervious to the developer. 'This needs attention. It will show in the print.'

As D.O. showed me to the door, he touched my shoulder lightly. 'If you are looking for a partner for the Highland Ball, there is one right here who offers affection and isn't impressed by novelty.'

How easy it would have been to stammer a breathless *Yes*, but I was resolved to engage my rational self rather than my emotions. 'I shall have to check my diary,' I said.

In the dimness of the hall, I could not see his expression, though his voice was level and unperturbed. 'Of course. But whoever you choose, make sure he is worthy of you.'

I wondered what art or artifice had brought us to this point and how much truth could be found in it.

With the onset of autumn Charles Eastlake wrote to me. On my last visit to London, this artist and scholar had proved a very agreeable companion. With the best grasp of the German language I had ever encountered in an Englishman, his wit and intelligence more than compensated for a lack of handsome features. All of which came back to me when I received his letter, explaining he was in Edinburgh and bore with him two books from Mr Lockhart for me to review; one was Thackeray's *Vanity Fair*, the other a more gothic composition by the mysterious Currer Bell. When Eastlake arrived, he said that as novels were not to his taste, he had read neither but had heard the heroines were of very different casts and knew Lockhart to be eager for my opinion.

I accepted his invitation to an evening at the home of mutual friends and found a degree of relief in the company of someone offering consummate courtesy without the complications of emotion. If there was a deeper attraction on his part, he was far too polite to allude to it, all of which made for the most relaxing form of society.

The cold of an Edinburgh winter is often exaggerated, but by the time Matilda's wedding had taken place in October, the dark days were upon us, remarkable not for frost but for the dismal veil of cloud which could dampen the strongest constitution.

Eastlake had departed and on evenings when there was no theatre or dinner to distract, I was left with only Becky Sharp and Jane Eyre for company, of whom the former, despite her flightiness, was much to my preference. There was so little to like about Jane and although she rose in the end to the difficulties of her situation, I challenge any woman to feel attracted to the boorish Mr Rochester. Before I was even half way through I had written to Mr Lockhart saying as much and refuting absolutely the notion of the mysterious author being a woman.

Robert Adamson, prey to his old afflictions, had gone home to Fife, bringing an end to that year's picture making. D.O., however, was as good as his word and his invitation to the Ball immediately dispelled any seasonal gloom. Great efforts were put into the choosing of my dress and stole and the dressing of my hair, although as the time approached I found the lightness of my heart tinged with unease.

'Don't you think he is going to make his feelings known?' Mama said, as she fastened my stole with a silver clasp.

D.O. had never been a man to hide his feelings. I did not think he would choose such a public occasion to profess something he had hidden so far. He was, however, most handsomely got up as a Highland Chief and it was no less a thrill than I expected to throw myself into the whirl of the dance, knowing what a fine pair we made as we sped around the floor.

In the interval, his friend Dr Bell found me in a quiet corner and said how happy D.O. looked in my company. 'And I in his,' I acceded, 'although I think D.O. is rarely gloomy in a crowded room.'

Bell laughed and said I was as clever as my reputation and he hoped I might become more than a dancing partner to his friend. I wondered if he would convey this thought to D.O. himself. Otherwise the evening passed in merriment with no great seriousness of conversation and I did not dwell on the remark, although it came to the forefront of my mind a few weeks later when I received an unexpected invitation from D.O., asking if I would call to collect something I had 'likely forgotten.' 'If you can manage Sunday after the kirk,' the note continued, 'we could also take the air on Calton Hill.'

He was at the garden gate with Charlotte beside him when I arrived. I had not reckoned on her taking the air with us, although she danced along happily enough, exclaiming at sights and sounds along the way and greeting other walkers whether she knew them or not, which occasioned D.O. to remind her that friendliness is not always welcome.

I found myself in sympathy with the child's impulsiveness. 'She is growing to a fine girl,' I said. My arm was in his and I felt no awkwardness in the little group we made, except I caught a look of worry in D.O.'s eyes even as he smiled at his bairn's antics.

'Something is troubling you?'

'Robert's heath is worse than ever. His brother, the doctor, writes to me every day.'

I encouraged him to optimism. 'It's just the winter coming on. He will be back to take more pictures for you, you will see.'

His face remained grave. 'I hope you're right. At any rate, it's a picture I have asked you to call for today.'

When we had wended our way back down to Rock House, he sent Chattie to the kitchen to see if there was a cake and took me to the back parlour where a calotype had been left propped on a bookshelf. It was the picture he had taken in the spring, the lovelorn maiden with her cherub, and where Mr Adamson had worried over the mark on the paper, someone had made a star, just above my shoulder.

He handed it to me. 'What do you think?'

I was well enough acquainted with such devices to know the implication of the star; a lover's keepsake was what it said, of course no more than we had imagined on that day. I was reluctant to read more into it and felt the need to tread carefully.

'A happy artifice,' I said.

He sighed and rubbed his hand through his hair. 'Is everything artifice to you, Elizabeth?'

I shook my head. 'I know you are a good-hearted man and an honest one,' I said. 'But your duty is to your art. Beauty is not always truth, nor truth beauty, whatever poets might say.'

We both caught sight of Charlotte in the doorway.

'No cake?' I asked, and she shook her little head in sorrow.

He lifted her into his arms, his face transformed by a father's smile. 'We aye have cake on a Sunday,' he said. 'I'll have to scold the cook.'

I was left holding the calotype.

'It's yours to keep,' he said 'I'm sorry it was forgotten for so long.'

'Thank you. I'll treasure it. It will be a souvenir . . . of my time in Edinburgh.'

We were both taken by surprise, myself no less than him.

He set Charlotte down. 'You are leaving?'

I tried to make light of it. 'London always calls,' I said.

A knock at the door presaged his other family arriving and I took my leave.

And so our dance was ended.

Edinburgh for all its delights was an interlude rather than a homecoming, and was it not better to be loved in absence than not loved at all? Charles Eastlake was the best suitor I could hope to find and I knew from his demeanour that his proposal was only a matter of time.

Until then, I would content myself with the company of Mr Thackeray and Mr Bell.

FADING

CHAPTER TEN

In the Shadow of the Door

Jane Adamson, St Andrews, January 1848

Robert was always the frailest and the most fussed over of my brothers. Every winter since I can remember, he has taken to his bed to be plied with beef tea and daubed with embrocation. The smell of it is in the fabric of the walls, mixed with polish and the steam of yesterday's soup.

After he went to live in Edinburgh, he still came home for the winter, which is why we thought this year the same as any other. The sickness was just a visitor who outstayed his welcome but always went on his way. We expected, come February, Rob would lever himself up on one elbow and ask if the burn was still frozen and how many hens had been lost. When the fever didn't subside, we told ourselves to be patient, trying not to hear his cough above the hissing of coals in the grate. Then, last week, John came to see him, furrowed his brows and said he would take him to St Andrews, to have him by his side. We should have known that something was amiss but we told ourselves it was the best thing. Rob would soon recover in his brother's care.

This time the visitor deceived us, or we deceived ourselves. Two days ago, John came back alone, slack-faced and bearing the worst news of all.

Mother, when she can find words, blames the weather: there has been too little frost, with the kale rotting at the root. In our hearts we know the weather is the least of it. We wonder if Rob should have come home sooner, or if he never should have gone to Edinburgh with its fancy ways and mucky streets.

At least he is home now. They brought him yesterday for his lying in and left the parlour door open so that his soul can come and go as it pleases. Today he'll be buried in St Andrews. When I woke I felt his gentle nature close to me and now, with the rest of the house barely stirring, I've come to pay my final respects.

I stop at the parlour door, the sight of the plain oak coffin hard enough to bear without going in and seeing his face, on its bed of crimson silk, reduced to an empty page.

The lightening sky casts a stray beam onto the calotype set on the mantelpiece. I step around the coffin to take the family portrait in my hands. John and Alexander stand behind, Robert in front bowed over the family bible. My sisters sit next to him. It was taken two summers ago by Mr Hill. Holding it to the light, I see Rob as young and as full of life as on the day it was made.

It was August, I remember, with the brambles ripening early. Rob and Mr Hill came from the town by the cliff path. The camera and everything they needed had already arrived by road. They would ride back afterwards in the gig, they said, to develop the picture as quickly as they could.

In the back room, the artist's smile flashed round the company. No taller than Rob, he filled the space around him. He was used to taking centre stage. He apologised for taking up our time and at short notice. 'But it's a fine day for a picture. Too good to miss, eh Rob?'

I was sent to bring out the best china but Mr Hill wouldn't take tea. Mother, in her widow's weeds, declared the picture would be 'just the bairns.' And so we were called to the garden, but I hung back in the doorway, watching the others shuffling about, moving to his bidding.

Rob called to me, 'Come on, Janie,' but I shook my head, reluctant to put on my best clothes and stand about like a gowk.

'There's always an awkward one,' John said, catching my eye and smiling. Mr Hill looked at me too, weighing me up, deciding to let it go. I was grateful for his forbearance and something kept me there, in the shadow of the door, watching while keeping my distance.

When the group was arranged to his satisfaction, Mr Hill bent down to peer through the lens. 'Rob, you must come here and tell me if you see what I see.'

He and Rob changed places so that Rob could look through the camera. Mr Hill took his place in the family group. It was only a matter of composition, of judging the light, of trying a pose, but seeing him in my brother's place sent a chill through me. Did I foresee the day when Rob would be gone?

As I lay the picture back on the mantelpiece there is a movement behind me. John is looking over my shoulder.

'I should have looked after him better.'

I turn to hold him by the shoulders and put my cheek against his. 'Nobody loved him more.' I wipe my eyes with the pinnie. 'I'll see to the breakfast.'

John holds my wrists. 'There's no hurry.'

With the light growing up from the sea and the pullets complaining in the yard, it could be any winter's morning. We stand beside the casket and I don't shy away from the pale blank face. For a last wee while the three of us are together.

'So will he come today?' I ask. I don't need to say his name, the Edinburgh friend. 'It's a good day's journey and I expect he has plenty to keep him down there.' Being as he is the famous artist, the important man.

John's hooded eyes are on the coffin. 'He'll be here. He'll

have taken the ferry last night and stayed this side of the water.'

I smooth my skirt and make to go past him but he puts his hand on my shoulder. 'D.O. mourns as deeply as any of us. I don't know why you've taken against him. He was like a brother to Rob.'

Rob had brothers already, I want to say, here in St Andrews. This new brother took him away from those who cared for him. But what would be the use? His brother is a doctor and still couldn't save him.

In the back room I wipe each knife and fork as I lay them on the breakfast table, rehearsing my resentment of D.O. Hill. 'You do all the work,' I said to Rob after the calotype was made, 'and he gets all the glory.'

Rob laughed and said D.O. brought in business and had a way with folk that got the best out of them. 'I can't be doing with all that becking and booing. You'll get to like him, Janie. Everybody likes him.'

John, Mother, Alexander and the girls come down and we sit close to one another around the table. Mother shrinks with the loss of every child. I force myself to eat my share because it'll be a long day and a cold one. My stomach growls at the onslaught.

The man whom everybody likes. Maybe you had to be in front of the camera for his magic to rub off. If so, I have missed my chance. If D.O. Hill came now, doffing his hat in the doorway, offering his condolences, would I make my peace? By the time the coffin leaves for St Andrews, the only caller is a widow from Boarhills who helped nurse Rob in winters past. There is no sign of a visitor from Edinburgh. Maybe he has missed his chance.

While the men are at the burial, the women lay out bread, cheese, cold ham and beef, at John's house in South Street, ready for the mourners when they come back from the kirk yard. Mother walks from the kitchen to the parlour and back again, asking what needs to be done but doing none of it, then sits down in a wing chair, exhausted by the weight of her black crepe. I slice potted meat onto an ashet, licking a fleck of jelly that falls from the bowl, tasting tears.

Melville, my youngest sister, looks at the clock. 'They won't be long,' she says. Straight away there are men's voices in the lobby and a draught from the front door paws at our ankles.

John is first and behind him Brewster, his jowls in a grimace of mourning. The women rise to greet him but he addresses only Mother. 'Mrs Adamson, you have my deep condolences.'

Mother looks past him to the crowd in the hall-way. 'Come away in and warm yourselves.' It's John's house but today she is the hostess, leaving her sons to dispense drams of whisky.

The men take off their hats and wait in line to shake her hand. Owners of neighbouring farms and shopkeepers from Cupar rub shoulders with the Provost, teachers and university men. Last in the line is D.O. Hill. He has kept his promise, even if it is too late.

He steps out of the line to come towards me. 'Miss Adamson, I'm sorry for your loss. He will be sorely missed.'

His fingers are as cold as the graveyard he's come from and I withdraw mine in shock. I remember him taller and younger, or maybe the sadness has diminished him as it has Mother.

'You will miss him too.' I can see it in his eyes and the shadows beneath them, as deep as bruises.

'I can't tell you how much.'

In my brother's parlour, it's Brewster and the provost who draw all the attention. One or two of the mourners nod to Mr Hill but no one beckons him to join their group.

'You are chilled,' I say. 'Let me get you a dram.'

He smiles when I bring him the whisky 'Thank you. It was gey dreich at the graveside.'

The family grave is under the cathedral towers. Where the

ruins give onto the headland, there is no shelter from the raw wind. I expect him to move away to speak to John but he stays beside me. I grope for words. 'You'll know Sir David?'

'And some of the others. They are in Edinburgh often enough.'

As we sit to the table, the question ripples through the farm folk, *Who is the stranger?* The answer goes round like the sigh of wind through barley. *The artist, he's come from Edinburgh.*

After the meal, Mr Hill and John stand together. 'I've asked D.O. to stay the night,' John says. 'He'll be too late for the ferry.'

He and John leaned into each other like stooks of corn against the rain.

'Come back to the farm,' I say. 'Mother would like to see you and hear more about what you and Rob were up to.' There are gaps in our memories left by Rob's Edinburgh years.

He shakes his head. 'I think my presence might only make things worse. But thank you.'

I don't press him, as he did not press me to be calotyped.

'We'll always have the picture you took. It's a fine thing, the best reminder we could have.'

'I wish there were more. Rob hardly ever sat for a picture.'

'And when he did, I was too cussed to join in.'

He allows himself a smile. 'Most folk I can persuade. Not all of them.'

Between us a silence falls containing nothing other than our shared memories and our sense of loss. I remember my Beatitudes. *Blessed are the peacemakers.* 'If only . . .'

He cuts me off. 'We all have our regrets. Myself included. So many things . . . so many times . . . '

John takes him by the arm. 'None of us can see the future. You're not to blame. None of us is to blame.'

John is right. I have known it all along, but sometimes you need to hurl your anger at something or somebody.

Hill's hand is on John's shoulder. 'Not you, John, never you. No one could have taken better care of him.'

They embrace. He is John's brother too.

He says he will leave on the next coach and stay the night with friends further south. As the lamps are lit, John and I stand at the front door to wish him goodbye.

He hurries down the street with his coat pulled around him, as if the east wind might take it from his back. Without Rob, there will be nothing to bring him here again.

Less than a week later, I am at the family grave with John standing next to me. Rob's name is freshly carved on the raw stone. The sun is back and the towers make sharp shadows across the grass. As we walked from South Street, he told me D.O. Hill had written, asking him to go to Edinburgh, to take Rob's place.

'I've decided against it,' he says.

I look into the diamond sky. 'I can't say I'm sorry.'

John puts his arm around my shoulders to shield me from the wind and the constant clawing of grief. 'You never did take to the calotypes.'

I took to Mr Hill in the end, just too late for it to make a difference. 'They have their place, I say, 'when they're done well.' I lay my head against John's arm. 'But I would rather have my brothers here at home.

CHAPTER ELEVEN

Hopes and Fears

May Mann, Edinburgh, March 1848

Yesterday my sister put on her coat and went up the hill. She had seen nothing of D.O or his household since Robert Adamson's funeral. 'I must speak to him,' she said.

I didn't blame her, though it would have been kinder if he had called on us, to share the sadness of the funeral and make an end of things between them, rather than have her go to him. There is no arguing D.O. Hill is an honest man with good intentions, but none of us is perfect.

Jessie came back white-faced and tight-lipped. It was a cold day but I didn't think this was the only reason for her pinched look. She had something over her arm, a man's coat by the look of it.

'It's just the old jacket Rob used in the workshop. There's still some wear in it. I said I'd give it to the Poor House.'

She sat down with the jacket on her lap and, though I had plenty of other things to be doing, I sat down with her. I knew how fond she had been of him, of his youth and his eagerness and all the things he had to teach her. I didn't blame her for hanging on to whatever remnant of Robert Adamson might be trapped in the weave of the worsted.

'You will miss him.'

'I will miss both of them.'

Something still rankled and Jessie would get to it in the end. She shook out the coat, folded it more tidily and put it back where it was, smoothing the fabric with her fingers. 'D.O. won't carry on with the calotypes.'

He had asked John Adamson to join them, she said, but he had declined. In a week or two he was marrying a local girl, a family friend. He would rather stay in St Andrews. I had never met John but I was pleased for him. Folk should take something from death. John Adamson had looked at his life and seen what he needed to do. For Jessie, though, it was too soon. She had been up at Rock House for so long, and had nowhere else to go. And very little to come back to.

I got up to poke the fire. 'You should have gone up for the funeral.'

The grave-side is no place for a woman but she could have met his other family. If she had gone to St Andrews, she wouldn't be sitting here clutching a worn-out jacket.

I gave her some soup in a bowl and she put the coat to one side as she supped it. I watched the colour seep into her face. Afterwards she went out to the lobby and hung the coat on the back of the door. The Poor House would have to wait.

If only there had been more for her to do at home, but I had got used to managing without her. Now she rattled about the place, picking up a book and putting it down again a dozen times a day. Our brother, Sandy, still brought his journals for her to read but she left them undisturbed on the chair in the lobby. I knew if I asked, she would say what was the point of learning more if she couldn't put it to use?

In the afternoons, we sometimes went walking. She'd seen little of the city in the last few years and said it was good to be reacquainted. From the way she stopped on every corner and looked around her, I thought she was most likely eyeing up a calotype, imagining Robert there with his camera.

'You are used to being busy,' I told her. 'All that time with your developing and rinsing. Maybe you'll have to take in washing instead.'

I thought she had taken my joke to heart when I found her on the back green with a rug thrown over the line, setting about it with a carpet beater. By now it was March.

'I know it's time for the cleaning,' I said, 'but you don't have to do it yourself.'

All the same it was a fine day and I'd come down with a basket of washing. I could see it was doing her good to be out there even if the rug might be flayed to a pulp. She stopped beating and pulled the thing off the line to make room for the clothes. When I had finished pegging them out, we rolled up the rug between us and manhandled it up the stairs where we sat down to get our breath back. Her hair had come loose and she reached up to tuck the stray locks back in. Jessie's hair would never behave itself and the familiar gesture made me smile and she smiled back.

'So what are you going to do? I asked her.

'I don't know, May. I really don't know.'

Sandy was the one to come up with the answer – or an answer that looked promising. There was a housekeeper position coming up with Andrew Balfour who ran a school for boys in Musselburgh. Balfour had a wife and daughter. As well as housekeeping, Jessie could help the girl's governess with teaching the natural sciences. Sandy had paved the way. The job was Jessie's if she wanted it.

'What do you think?' Sandy asked.

It was perfect as far as I could see. 'You like sea air. And the change will do you good.' I could picture Jessie teaching the girl all the things she knew about the world, maybe even teaching in the school, but I left it there. Jessie had a cussed streak and too much encouragement was likely to push her the other way. Sandy said the girl, Isabel Balfour, was bright and would be good company. We were all thinking of Chattie Hill.

She too had been stolen from Jessie because of Robert's death.

'All right,' Jessie said. 'I'll go and see them. Maybe we'll suit each other.'

I could feel Sandy's relief meeting my own. In Jessie's eyes there was something like defeat.

A few days later she still hadn't been to see the Balfours and came in from the baker's cart with a half loaf under her arm and a new light in her eye.

'So will we go to Musselburgh?' I said. 'There's a coach at two o'clock.'

As she unpinned her hat, she shook her head. I couldn't make out the reason for a frown creasing her forehead. 'I just bumped into D.O. He's asked us up the hill this afternoon.'

In all the time Jessie had been visiting Rock House, I had been no farther than the doorstep, delivering a message or calling for her on the rare occasions she was needed at home. I was included in this invitation only for politeness and could easily have declined. But curiosity brought me here, to see the house where so much had taken place and to know the real purpose of this invitation: I could tell even Jessie didn't think it was just a social call. As we came up the steps, we passed the courtyard they had used as their studio, emptied of its chairs and statues. It had always been left bare in winter, surely this year the furnishings would not come out again, surely Jessie would not be pressed back into service.

D.O. was still on his way back from the town and we were shown into the parlour to wait.

'It's a fine room,' I said, craning my neck to see Arthur's Seat through a stubborn haar, thinking Jessie would be at home here amongst the brocade armchairs. She put me right straight away. 'Don't imagine I spent my time in the best room. I was always out the back or in the courtyard.'

We heard the front door open and D.O. conversing with the maid. Soon he came into the parlour, bearing the tea-tray himself. If anything my anxiety for Jessie grew stronger.

Sure enough, after some harmless pleasantries, he put his cards on the table. 'I need your help, Jessie. I have a commission to paint a new railway viaduct.' He paused to drink his tea, or to make a final decision. 'I'm getting too old to go sketching out of doors. What would you think about taking some calotypes?'

Calotypes. The word struck the air like an anvil on stone. If he had asked me, I would have told him not to bother my sister with another wild scheme when she was getting over the last one. But I was only here for appearance's sake.

Jessie, to give her her due, took her time over answering. She reached for a triangle of shortbread and broke it in two and two again.

D.O. was surprised at her hesitation. 'I thought you'd be keen to get back to it!'

Jessie still didn't rush to accept. She had come farther than I had realised in the past months.

'I'm not planning to run a studio,' he said. 'It won't be like before.' A fool could see it would never be like before. 'It's just this one time, unless, I suppose . . .'

Now she gave him a straight look and I read her mind. Unless what? Unless it went better than he hoped? And if it did, what would happen then? D.O. was a famously busy man with a picture still to finish for the Kirk. Surely the calotypes, for all the commotion they made, were only ever a distraction.

With D.O. failing to finish the thought that had us so perplexed, Jessie gave up her dissection of the shortbread which was just as well for the carpet square, already dusted with sugar from her plate.

'Every now and then there's a place for calotyping, Jessie. And this is one of them.' This was how he would speak to the members of his Academy when he was trying to get his way. Or was he trying to convince himself?

'And a man and his family must eat, ye know!'

Jessie's eyes softened to a smile. 'How is Chattie? I don't hear her about the place.'

He said she was out with his sister, that soon she'd be going to the college with her cousins. He laid down his cup and leaned towards Jessie, playing his final card.

'I've promised to do the viaduct this summer and I can't make calotypes on my own. We were always pals, you and me. Could you bear my company for a day or two?'

He was offering what they had shared before; the comradeship and the friendship.

Jessie was wavering. I wondered if she was reading more into his offer.

'Well, I suppose a day or two wouldn't hurt.'

'It will be a week at the most. I knew you wouldn't let me down.'

I resigned myself to this new scheme. With any luck it needn't interfere with the matter of the Balfours. 'So when will you begin?' I asked.

'I'll tell Boyd Alexander to expect us as soon as the weather settles. His family are good company, I promise.'

The name meant nothing to me, or, as far as I could see, to Jessie. A suspicion came over me. The railway was spreading its tentacles far and wide.

'So which viaduct are we talking about?'

'Ballochmyle, in Ayrshire. The railway passes through the estate at Mauchline. I know it well.'

It would be a full day's journey to Glasgow and beyond. I waited for Jessie to object, to say she couldn't possibly go so far and to folk she had never met. My sister, however, had chosen this moment to eat the remnants of the biscuit which she washed down with the last of her tea. When she'd got rid of the final mouthful, she said, 'I hear Ayrshire is very bonny. How exactly will we get there?'

As we walked back down the hill, I had lost the power of speech and Jessie likely knew that silence from me was the best she was likely to get. As we turned into our street, she drew a breath and announced that since the haar had gone and the days were lengthening, she would take a walk. I followed her like a dog after its master, only just keeping up with her lengthening stride. We'd walked past the Canongate Kirk and through the narrow streets to Dumbiedykes before either of us spoke.

'I suppose you think I shouldn't go.'

'I think he takes advantage of your good nature.'

'And is it such a bad thing, to offer him help when he needs it? He can't do it himself, you know. He never did learn the developing.'

We had left the buildings and arrived on the new road with the crags ahead of us. In the mood she was in, I wondered if we'd be clambering up the rock face, arguing all the way. The question in my mind was why he needed Jessie's help now.

'Could he not just sketch the viaduct? He must still do some drawing. Or he could ask somebody else to do it.'

She shook her head. 'He would need to be there, to see it first hand.'

She slowed down and we turned back towards Holyrood. The air was calmer here with more birdsong in it than soot. 'I don't know why he wants calotypes now,' Jessie said. 'Maybe there are reason he didn't mention.'

Jessie always had a soft spot for D.O. Did she think they would come back as more than friends? I had thought the Balfours would bring her freedom from all of this. I did not want her trammeled like a sparrow in the net of D.O.'s ill-conceived plans.

'What about Musselburgh?'

'We'll be in Ayrshire for a week at the most. Musselburgh will keep.'

'They might find somebody else.'

'In that case, I'll have to do the same.'

Once Jessie makes up her mind she sticks to it. I still worried over where one or both of them thought it would lead. When they came back, would she still be ready to find herself some new employment? Or did she think some other future would take shape? That was a thought best kept to myself.

'So you're off to stay with the Ayrshire gentry.'

Jessie could read my mind as well as I could read hers. 'I have seen plenty of gentry over the years. I can fit in as long as they are civil. He'll say I'm an old friend who helps him with his calotypes and they will take him at his word.'

D.O. had already asked her to go to Rock House and make all the preparations. She was telling me what would need to be done, talking to the air above the Pentlands as much as to me. I made a note to look out her best frocks and give them a good brushing down. Her only thoughts were for the camera and all it entailed.

It was cool and bright now, the haar long gone. I only wished my sister's future was as clear as the sunlit sky.

CHAPTER TWELVE

The Braes of Ballochmyle

May 1848

Jessie threw up the blinds in the workshop, blinking in the unaccustomed light. Last time she had stood here, the glass had been fingered with frost and her heart had been numb. With D.O.'s plan to go to Ayrshire, the numbness, like the frost, had thawed. Standing here in Rob's old space, the feelings that returned were no easier to bear, but bear them she must.

Rob had left it tidy, the sinks were empty and the old washing lines bore nothing but redundant pegs. Without thinking, Jessie rubbed her thumb across the fingers of the other hand, a habit that would never shift the black stain from her fingertips. It had never concerned her they would stay that way; neither had she expected to pick up the silvered sheets again and make her fingers blacker still. But if D.O. was set on calotyping, she couldn't refuse, for Robert's sake, for all of their sakes.

There was a footstep outside and D.O. appeared in the door. He was standing against the light and Jessie could see only his shape.

'You got here before me. Is there much we need to buy?'

She could see there was hypo and plenty of the iodising chemicals. 'I'll have to see how much paper we have. Will you take the big camera?'

He said Yes, the view of the viaduct would need the bigger lens, then he came into the room and sat down. His head was bowed under some new weight of grief.

'You haven't been out here since November, since Rob . . .?'

D.O. shook his head. 'I had no need to.'

She knew there was only one remedy for sorrow. 'We should make a start,' she said. 'We could be leaving any day. Go to the press and bring what paper we have.'

She took stock of the other supplies, discarding the bottles with only dregs left in, seeing with some surprise how little needed replacing. She could hardly believe it was only a few months since Rob had worked here.

She explained as she made up the iodising solution, 'Wait for the colour to clear, apply it as evenly as you can but leave the edge bare for handling.'

The paper would dry to palest primrose and keep its properties for months. As she worked through a dozen sheets, her hands moved more smoothly and the blood ran quicker in her veins. She had done it so often with Rob at her side. Maybe it was time for her to step up to the mark, to be the bearer of what he knew.

D.O. watched her closely but didn't offer to join in.

'He'd be proud of you, Jessie,' he said.

By the end of that week, the last shred of mist had left the Forth and Arthur's seat showed off its chiselled nooks and crannies against a brazen sky. A letter came from Mauchline saying D.O. and Jessie should come as quickly as they could.

The day before they left, D.O. fetched out the camera from its corner and Jessie ran a soft duster over it, bringing out the grain of the wood. D.O. laid his hand on it, a mark of respect, Jessie thought, saying farewell to an old friend in the best way there was, by continuing what he had begun.

It was a day's journey requiring two trains. From Edinburgh to Glasgow Jessie worried for their precious cargo stashed in the guards van while D.O. read a book, chuckling at familiar passages. From Kilmarnock, he hummed a tune under his breath.

'Rabbie Burns country, Jessie. We'll have a song one of those nights. The Alexanders are aye ready for a song.'

In the gloaming, his teeth flash a smile. She could feel the lightening of his heart.

The night air was soft when they got down from the train and were taken to Kingencluech House, home to D.O.'s friends and closer to the viaduct than Ballochmyle itself. They were warmly welcomed by Boyd Alexander and his wife Sophia. Jessie saw the equipment unloaded and slept well despite the unaccustomed quiet of the countryside and the strangeness of the bed.

Next morning, after breakfast, in a room that was more homely than grand, D.O. said they would calotype the viaduct from the river bank below.

'It might be harder than you think to get your apparatus down there,' Boyd said. 'The path is slippy even in summer. I can get one of the farm boys to give you a hand, if you give me an hour or two.'

D.O. considered this along with the remains of his egg. 'Jessie and I will go first, to spy out the land. If it's too difficult, we'll come straight back up, otherwise send your boy after us.'

Boyd was happy with this. Tonight, he said, some friends, were joining them for dinner. 'We can show them what you've done.'

Jessie excused herself. A room had been provided at the back of the house with a red curtain over the window. Here she made up the solution to give the paper its final treatment before it was put in the camera. The coating was sensitive to light: gallic acid, silver nitrate with acetic acid. Even in this unfamiliar place, it soothed her to be measuring, mixing, brushing and blotting. She swithered about adding to the strength of the gallic acid and wondered what Robert would say. It was summer and the light was good. She would leave it as it was. She set a sheet of the coated paper into each of the three dark slides and put some extra sheets in the printing frames, wrapping them in a length of dark worsted where they would stay as clean, damp and untainted by light as the others.

When D.O. came to find her, they packed everything on a handcart for the boys to bring after them. Sophia Alexander took Jessie to the back lobby where she rummaged in a kist full of old boots. 'No point in spoiling those shoes,' she said.

At the end of Kingencleuch drive, they stopped where a narrow bridge crossed a railway cutting. D.O. had borrowed a walking stick and pointed with it to where the ditch curved out of sight. The viaduct was just beyond a line of trees.

The path down was as steep as Boyd had predicted and dark, any light filtering through the leaves absorbed by red rocks on either side, leaving a soft mulch under foot. In boots that were a shade too big, Jessie picked her way down, grabbing at tussocks to prevent a fall.

D.O. came back and took her arm, laughing an apology. 'I'd forgotten it was so rough down here. Take my arm and we'll gang the gither."

Together they made better progress. Where the trees grew thinner, the banks were dappled with sun and starry clumps of celandines. As the path leveled out, Jessie stopped to shake moss from her gloves and get her breath back. He took her arm again as they carried on. 'You see,' he said, 'we'll manage after all.'

On the last descent, he began to sing a refrain of *The Lass of Ballochmyle*. Jessie recognised it as the tune he had been humming on the train. Boyd's aunt, he said, claimed to have met the poet in these very woods.

The air was heavy from the musty undergrowth. Jessie felt the warmth of it fill her lungs and thought how it would be fine to walk here again, by D.O.'s side, without the niggling worry of how much light would penetrate the trees and illuminate the viaduct they had come all this way to see.

When they stepped out onto the river bank, the flash of a kingfisher's wings across the water brought her back to the matter in hand. A spit of shingle stretched into the river which glimmered and burbled over a shallow silvery bed. D.O. walked on to the spit where he planted his stick and extracted it. Apparently satisfied with the firmness of the shingle, he waved to Jessie. 'Come and see the view.'

From this vantage point, the viaduct arches, hidden on their descent, towered over them. The brash newness of the stone couldn't take away from its majesty. A dozen trains a day would eventually rumble across it but for now it had the silent grandeur of a cathedral.

'What do you think?'

'I think Robert should have been here to see it.' He had loved the world around him; churches, railways and trees had taken his eye as much as the many faces in front of his camera.

D.O. put his hand on her shoulder. 'We must do it justice, then,' he said.

There was a movement at the top of the bank. Jessie could just make out an arm waving through the trees followed by a whistle and a shout. The cart had arrived. Ten minutes later after a deal of crashing and grumbling, the group stood together on the shingle, Jessie, D.O., the boy with his cart and Boyd Alexander himself, his shirt sleeves rolled above his elbows, wiping his forehead with a kerchief pulled from his waistcoat pocket.

'Well that was a sair fecht. I hope you're going to make my trip worthwhile.'

As soon as D.O. set the camera on the shingle, he was displeased. 'It's unsteady,' he said. 'Let's try farther up.'

There was a rocky ledge a short way up the bank and closer to the viaduct. D.O. hauled the camera up and Jessie followed.

Here the lilting melody of the river was muted to a low gurgle and the viaduct was mostly hidden by leafy shrubs clustered on the sandstone embankment. Jessie touched D.O.'s sleeve as he looked through the lens from under the cloth. She felt his indecision.

'Surely this isn't the view you want to paint?'

She took his silence for agreement.

'There's a good view from the other side of the viaduct,' he said when he had emerged, 'but it's a long way round, three miles at least from the house.'

It would mean going back up and starting again, or waiting till the next day. Boyd, still down by the water, was calling out encouragement, waiting for magic to be made. D.O. steadied the camera then stood aside to let Jessie look.

'What do you think?'

She had rarely got under the cloth to look through the lens and never grown accustomed to a world made back-to-front and upside-down. She struggled to make out if the trees were obscuring the view or adding to it.

D.O. was restless. 'Will we carry on or try again tomorrow, from the other side?'

The air was growing more humid and the light more milky than gold. Jessie's plain frock, chosen to withstand brambles down the path, felt as heavy as sack-cloth and irked her around the neck and under her arms.

'It feels like thunder to me,' she said. 'I think we should give it a try.' If the weather broke, they could be stymied.

D.O. went back to the camera. 'And what exposure?'

Jessie didn't deal with exposing – only with the results. When the men had gone out to take pictures, she had usually waited at Rock House. If Rob had been here now, he would have looked at the sky and told them what to do but however hard and long Jessie stared into the space between the river and the sky, Robert failed to materialise.

The farm boy started up a tuneless whistle and began

throwing stones in the river. Boyd had fallen silent like a spectator at some entertainment, wondering if the show was ever going to start. D.O. had one hand on the camera, the other in his waistcoat, feeling for his watch. Jessie had to decide.

'There's a haze but the light is still good,' she said, trying not to hear the bravado in her voice. 'We'll do three different exposures. From those we'll know if anything needs to be changed for another time.'

D.O. inserted each slide, removed it and replaced it with another as Jessie timed the exposure, penciling it on the back of each one. When everything was brought down and packed away, D.O. smiled at his audience, apparently confident of his and Jessie's efforts.

'You see, that's all it takes. Jessie will do the developing for us. She'll have something to show us by dinner time.'

Bravado, it seemed, was infectious.

She had been right not to trust the weather. By the time they were back at the house, the haze had dimmed to bronze and clouds were bulking the western sky. The other visitors were expected at four and so the men went to change and take tea with them. In the red dusk of the dark-room, Jessie checked the curtain for chinks of light and took the first negative from its slide. She was happy to be alone with Rob's ghost for company.

The developing solution was a combination of the two sensitising liquids. He had taught her to spread each of them across the negative, using a swab of cotton rather than a brush. She had hit on the idea of immersing the slide in the developer so that none of the image would be missed. She did it now in her own way, in Rob's company, but without his help.

Folk thought that magic was quick and science was slow but Robert had liked to surprise them. 'The picture is there already,' he would say to visitors. 'It takes no longer to develop it than it does for it to form in the paper.' He also reminded them that even after years of practice, a lot could go wrong.

She watched each image appear. The negatives were blurred. The viaduct arches were lost behind the trees and the trees themselves were a muddied mass. She had been flustered by the presence of Boyd Alexander and in too much of a hurry to get results. It was the wrong picture to take and she had done it poorly. Seeing the results, she knew all the exposures were wrong. Robert had delighted in catching the effect of light on foliage. These negatives were a waste of time and paper.

At the front door she could hear voices raised in greeting. She washed out the developer, applied the hypo, washed the calotypes again twice over. Her hope drained away with the last of the rinsing water. Nothing could make these negatives better.

In the doorway of the parlour, Jessie paused. The new arrivals were a handsome couple in their middle years and with them a younger woman. The company, with Boyd and Sophia, were seated in a semi-circle. D.O. stood at its centre, regaling them with the story of their journey to the river and how they had all but fallen in at the foot of the bank. Remonstrating, Boyd got up to join him and put his arm around D.O.'s shoulder. 'Don't believe everything he tells you. He looked perfectly dry to me until he chose to wade in the water looking for trout.'

The story was gathering a momentum of its own. Jessie was a stranger here and about to cast a shadow over their merriment. She would have left and saved the calotypes for later but D.O. spotted her and called her in. She apologised for the lack of clarity in the negatives, explaining to the company how many things could have made a difference, the strength of the sensitiser, the position of the camera on the bank.

D.O. cut her off, seeing, just before she did, the polite but blank indifference in the eyes of the visitors and Boyd's irritation at the lack of a fitting climax to his story.

'Well,' D.O. said, 'we're missing our old colleague. He was the one with the real expertise.'

139

Jessie felt a blade of hurt steal under her ribs. She was trying her best. With time, she could learn.

Boyd clapped D.O. on the shoulder. 'Maybe you'll just have to get out your pencil and paper and be a proper artist.'

'Aye, aye,' D.O. said, 'there's more than one way to make a picture, right enough.'

If Robert had been there, D.O. would have talked of art and light and Rembrandt. Jessie, who had come down without changing from her working clothes, slipped out of the room, saying nothing.

Jessie needn't have worried about changing since her best lace was more than outdone by the crimson finery of Mrs Stenhouse who sat next to her at dinner. Marion Smythe, her sister, was more quietly dressed in a blue and grey plaid that brought out her auburn hair and blue-green eyes. Jessie watched as D.O. brought the younger woman out of her shell until his compliments turned her fair complexion a pearly pink. He then entertained the company with the story he had told her by the river of Rabbie Burns, asking Boyd if his aunt really had been the inspiration for the song.

'She certainly dined out on the story,' Boyd said. 'Whether it was true or not.'

The discussion became animated but Jessie was unmoved. In this formal dining room, the Alexander family looked down on her from gilded frames as she reviewed the mistakes she might have made with the calotypes. With D.O. leaving everything to her bar the taking of the picture, it was clear their failure lay at her door. Remembering the walk to the river and the lush undergrowth on the bank and path, she realised it was unlikely ever to dry out, even in a heat-wave. The moisture must have caused a reaction in the iodised paper, calling for a different dilution of the initial preparation or of the sensitiser. She needed to understand it better and work out how to redress the balance.

When the storm broke in a flash of lightning and a great crack of thunder, Jessie was jolted from her reflections in time to hear Marion Smythe cry out and to see D.O. reach for the girl's hand. 'There there, it's just the weather gods having a wee falling out.'

Sophia stood up and folded her napkin. 'We should go through,' she said. 'We can forget the wind and weather with a song.'

In the parlour, D.O. was first on his feet with Marion at the piano. Jessie had forgotten what a fine voice he had. Mr Smythe, in the next chair to Jessie, leaned over. 'And do you sing, Miss Mann?'

Jessie shook her head. With Sandy or with May, maybe, but not here in this company. For his next song, D.O. invited the girl to join him. Her voice was sweet and low and gained in confidence as they began the second verse.

Next morning, the rain had stopped beating on the windows but the sky was overcast. Jessie berated herself for her lingering bad temper: the sun would return sooner or later; there would be other days for calotyping, and the visitors, invited to stay the night on account of the weather, would soon be gone. In the darkroom, the windows had been closed tight against the storm and the air was sour. Jessie preferred to be here rather than take another meal in company.

It was an hour before D.O. came to find her and for once she wished he had not. 'We missed you at breakfast, Jessie. Is anything amiss?'

She was giving the calotypes a final wash. 'Only the weather,' she said. 'Though if it dries up, I can print these and give you something to show for yesterday.'

She was bending over a basin of water and sensed his presence at her shoulder. She felt a need to break the silence. 'Will we try the view from the east side today, do you think?'

He moved away as he spoke and lifted the curtain to look

out at the brightening sky, 'I don't think so. If the rain stays away, as the gillie says it will, we're all taking a picnic to the woods, with the visitors and the bairns, maybe ending at Barskimming.' This was what she had missed at breakfast. 'Boyd's brother will join us from the big house. You're invited of course.'

William Alexander was the Laird. Jessie was here only as D.O.'s assistant, above the gillie and the farm boy, but only on the fringes of the company.

'That's very kind,' she said without turning round. 'But I think I'll stay here. And the calotypes?'

'Maybe tomorrow. Let's wait and see.'

His voice held no conviction.

While they were gone, and with the house falling silent, Jessie roamed the downstairs rooms until she found the Kingencleuch library. She pushed open the heavy door and went inside, hoping for a chemistry book or even some scientific papers to help her work out what to try next with the calotypes. Walking from shelf to shelf she could see only novels or biblical texts and with nothing better to do, sat down at a table bearing London magazines and a single heavy volume. The magazines contained stories and she flicked through them for a while although none held her interest. When she opened the book, the title page read, 'The Land of Burns, a series of landscapes and portraits, illustrative of the life and writings of The Scottish Poet.' The landscapes were from paintings by D.O. Hill Esq, R.S.A. This was what had brought him here before. The date was 1840, nearly twenty years ago.

She turned a few pages and examined the first few plates. Barskimming was a stretch of water not unlike the bend in the river they had seen the day before with its steep banks and overhanging trees, spanned by a high arched bridge. This is where they were having their picnic, but she was happy enough to see these places through his eyes and in the fine lines his fingers had made.

She must have dozed off in the warmth and solitude. She was woken by D.O.'s voice and his head around the door.

'They said you were hiding in here. Am I disturbing you?'

She shook herself and rubbed her hand over her face. The more she felt herself in a house of strangers, the more she welcomed his company. She motioned to the seat next to hers. 'Look. I'm traveling without leaving the room.'

He saw the book, open somewhere in the middle, and laughed. 'I can't recommend a better companion. Unless the man who wrote it.'

'Then why don't you tell me yourself?'

The text alongside the plates was by some professor. D.O. sat down and gave her his own version, starting from the beginning, stopping at each plate to recount his memories of how the weather had been, where he had stayed and which landscapes pleased him the most. The warmth of the room and the comfort of his voice lay over Jessie like a finely knitted shawl.

'From Tarbolton to Mauchline is the finest stretch of the Ayr,' he said, and even in her half-sleep she caught a wistfulness in his voice.

'1840,' she said. 'So was Ann here with you?'

The silence lengthened. He shook his head. 'Two summers I was here, sitting in the damp with my sketch pad when I could have been with my wife at my own fireside.'

She reached for his hand on the open book and covered it with hers. 'You had your work to do. And you made good friends here who love you still.'

'You've been as good a friend as any, Jessie.'

But he took his hand away and went back to the book, turning over the last few pages, smiling to himself over some tale of mischief at Tarbolton Cross.

As he closed the book, he flexed the fingers Jessie knew were plagued with rheumatism. This had been the first cause of it, the reason sketching and sometimes painting cost him dear.

'I have let you down with the calotypes,' she said. 'I can do better.'

Now he was the one to reach for her hand. 'You have done wonders, Jessie, and maybe there are others who will give you work. There are plenty more calotypists these days. You must decide for yourself.' He sat back in his chair, his eyes never leaving hers. 'But I am done with it.'

The truth was like the tolling of a bell. Maybe she had known it all along and pretended it was otherwise for his sake. Maybe he had done exactly the same, offering her a new beginning while doubting it would ever come to pass.

He was examining his fingers again. Unlike Jessie's, they were unmarked by the silver salts. 'Boyd is right. These hands will have to suffice and they are not so bad that I can't make the sketches I need.' He reached into an inside pocket. 'You weren't the only one to refuse the picnic. When I left you today I went down to the viaduct and made a start.'

'From the other side?'

He smiled his old smile and handed her a sheet of paper. 'No, from the very place we stood yesterday. Where Boyd would have them think I went looking for trout.'

He had placed only a few lines on the paper, but enough to suggest the viaduct rising from the trees. 'Your calotypes will never hang in a gallery, but they still helped me see the best view.'

As the sun dropped at the window behind him, it lit the gilded spines of the books on the opposite wall. 'So sometimes the old ways are best,' Jessie said. 'You'll need a few more days, I expect.'

D.O. leaned forward, his hands on his knees, as if he was already planning his next expedition to the river. 'You're welcome to stay. Sophia is fond of you. She and the bairns enjoy a change of company.'

Jessie stretched out her legs. She could have stayed a while longer here, in the library, with D.O. telling her about the old times. Even May would not begrudge her that. But he didn't need her help.

'I am the one who needs a change of company,' she said. 'I can take the camera back for you and put it away where it belongs. I'm glad to have seen Ayshire, but it's time I went home.'

NEW PROCESSES

CHAPTER THIRTEEN

All His Darlings

Chattie Hill, Edinburgh, 1855

All of my life, folk have come to our house and asked when will my faither take another wife. And he has always said Ann, my mother, was the only wife he ever wanted and I am all the company he needs.

Now I am nearly sixteen and I think there is maybe a difference between having company and having a wife, which is why I take note when Uncle Noel Paton comes to talk to me about his sister, Amelia.

Uncle Noel is only a distant relative but he comes here very often and when he's away, he writes my faither letters which make him laugh out loud and sit down to write back straight away, even though they will be seeing each other within a day or two.

My faither says Noel has enough life in him for two people and he certainly takes up double the space of most. His curly red hair flies around when he talks, putting me more in mind of some jungle creature than an artist whose brushwork, Dada says, is the best you will ever see.

He creeps up on me one day when I am curled up behind the curtain on the window-seat, reading my book. He is as light on his feet as a kitten.

'How's my favourite niece today?' he says, as he sits down next to me. I say I am fine and enjoying the Ladies College which is the kind of thing uncles like to hear. I can feel the rise and fall of his breathing. Years ago I used to lean against his tweedy flank for comfort; now I would rather stay in the pages of my book but from his manner I guess he has something important to say and so I close it, keeping one finger in to mark my page.

'Do you remember my sister, Amelia?' he asks which of course I do, although we haven't seen her for a while.

He pokes me in the ribs with his elbow and says she will be calling more and is looking forward to seeing more of me and my Dada. Out of politeness I smile and say that will be nice. Uncle Noel beams as if I have said exactly the right thing

I have never called Amelia 'Auntie,' though I like her well enough, even if she is not so vivacious as Noel. Dada says Amelia, like her brother, has an artist's blood in her veins but has not had the time to develop her talent. This makes me wonder what makes an artist. Amelia has none of Noel's flamboyance but then Dada's paintings are quiet things that look fine on a parlour wall whereas Noel's need a great space to contain them.

Dada asks if I remember how Amelia once took me to the burn behind their house and only just managed to stop me from falling in. I don't remember but it feels like the kind of thing Amelia would do, whereas Uncle Noel would have jumped in the burn with me and got us both soaking wet.

Amelia is small and serious and very keen on Nature which she says has everything to teach us about God's Creation. One day, she asks if I would like to go with her to the Museum in Chambers Street. We are in the gallery inspecting some fossils, when two women come round the corner arm in arm.

One is our old friend, Jessie Mann, who used to live close by but has moved away to Musselburgh. Without thinking, I run up to her and give her a hug.

She steps away to look at me, her eyes twinkling, because we have always been good pals and introduces her companion, a young woman of nineteen or so called Isobel Balfour.

I introduce Jessie to Amelia, explaining how she was a great help to Dada when he and Robert were making their famous calotypes. At this Isobel becomes very animated. 'Does your faither still take the pictures? You wouldn't believe how much I'd like to have one!'

I think of my Dada as an old man but I know most ladies think otherwise and from the pink in Isobel's cheeks, I see she is no different. Jessie gives me a look, as if to apologise for Isobel's enthusiasm.

I smooth my skirt and think how a young lady should reply. 'Faither is very busy and rarely makes calotypes but maybe you could write to him and ask.'

'Oh we will,' Isobel says. 'Won't we, Jessie?'

As we walk back over the North Bridge, I ask Amelia if it's true that she would like to be an artist. She waits for a lull in the noise of carts and carriages and says it's something she has thought about but has still to settle on her true vocation.

I tell her I think she would be good at drawing Nature.

'Well, everything that's art is in nature,' Amelia says, which puzzles me until I realised that people are part of nature too.

'You sound like Faither,' I say.

'Well, he would be the one to know,' she says with one of her rare smiles, by which I think she means that Dada has copied nature in very many ways.

Next time he and I are together, I tell him I find Cousin Amelia, as I now call her, a good companion with interesting opinions.

He looks at me narrowly. 'Well thank you,' he says, 'I will bear it in mind if I am ever in any doubt.'

This tells me nothing and so I carry on. 'And I think Isobel Balfour will soon be writing to ask you for a calotype.'

He runs his hand through his hair in a way that signifies

weariness. 'And do you have an opinion of Miss Balfour?'

This is too good an opportunity to miss. 'Well, she is very bonny and bright, but in terms of intellect, not a patch on Cousin Amelia.'

This makes him roar with as much laughter as if he was reading one of Noel's letters, but when his laughter subsides he heaves a sigh. Any mention of calotypes brings back the sadness he still feels at the death of his dear friend, Robert, and this is another reason to make sure he has the right kind of company.

Our other new visitor is Mr Brodie, the sculptor, who is making a bust of me to celebrate my sixteenth birthday. Dada has sent him sketches so that he knows just how I look from every angle but he has asked to come to see me for himself and perhaps do more drawings. When he arrives, Dada is out but Amelia is with us and says would I like her to sit with me during the sketching, which is kind of her as I have never sat for anyone other than Dada.

We go into the front parlour where the light is good and I sit in front of the window looking to the side. Amelia has some sewing with her which she often brings but mostly she sits quietly, watching and listening.

Mr Brodie has rosy cheeks and an accent which he brought from Aberdeen but is not long back from studying in Italy. I ask him about Rome and Florence. He says they are wonderful and I should go there when my father can spare me. Afterwards, Amelia says we should go down Princes Street and look at the statues on the Scott Monument, some of which have been made by Mr Brodie. I am still surprised how knowledgeable Amelia is about every kind of art.

When Uncle Noel next comes, he doesn't bring Amelia but talks to Dada about the Great Painting which he has still not finished. Dada calls it a millstone round his neck and Uncle Noel says the only way to cast it off is to finish it quickly and he would help Dada with it if only it wasn't so very far from his own style of painting.

Later, I pull Uncle Noel's sleeve and tell him I have spent some fine times with Cousin Amelia and how we all enjoy her company. 'Since Amelia would like to be an artist, maybe she could help Dada with the Great Painting.'

Then Uncle Noel puts his arm around my shoulder and gives me a squeeze. 'You are a fine girl, Chattie, and love your father dearly but I think in the matter of the painting he may be beyond help.'

Summer has arrived and we go on an outing to Dunfermline and take a picnic to the hills, the party being made up of Dada, my cousins from Rock House, Amelia, her father and two of her cousins from Fife. We take carriages all the way to Saline then walk up a long hill. At the top where we stop for our picnic there's a bonny view of the Ochils on one side and the Forth on the other and no sound except the call of linnets and fieldfares.

When we have eaten, I see that Faither and Amelia are having some long discussion about Mr Brodie and his sculptures so I collect up the cousins and the Dunfermline people and say. 'With so many blaeberries about, why don't we pick some to take home?'

This takes us all in different directions across the hill, seeking out the purple berries that hide so meanly amongst the leaves, leaving Dada and Amelia to be private if they so wish.

My cousin Ann and I are last to come back to our picnic place, by which time everybody is packing up, but both Amelia and Faither are in good spirits and I hope there has been time enough for them to conclude their private business. I'm only sorry I can't report on any of this to Uncle Noel, who has gone off to see his artist friends in London.

That night, Dada says I'm to call on Mr Brodie so that he can make finishing touches to his model which will then be used to cast a bronze in my likeness. 'I will take you there on Monday afternoon,' he says, 'after College.'

Because it's a stretch from the New Town to Mr Brodie's house, we go in the carriage, 'to save my old legs,' Dada says. He has work to do at the Academy and will collect me later.

As we rattle along Princes Street, I ask him if he enjoyed speaking to Cousin Amelia on the picnic and he says that it was a very fine day and it's a pity we don't get more of them. He also asks what I'm studying in College and for my own pleasure and says he hopes I am sticking to the great books of Sir Walter and not getting lost in the cheap novels he sees my cousins reading. I'm not sure what caused this remark but I can tell him honestly that I haven't had much time for reading lately as I have had other things to think about. He says he hopes they are sensible things worthy of the young lady he knows I am.

When we arrive at Cambridge Street, Mrs Brodie welcomes me in and leaves me with the bairns until Mr Brodie is ready. They have a new kitten and as it scampers up the curtains and across the rugs, I forget the real reason for my being there until Mr Brodie calls me in.

Since I know Mr Brodie now, I have told Dada I'll be fine on my own, so I am very surprised when I go into Mr Brodie's studio to find Cousin Amelia is there before me. I greet her and say I hadn't expected to see her today.

She smiles. 'And I didn't know you were calling, otherwise I would have sent a note.'

My bust is on a table in the centre of the room. Cousin Amelia is standing by another table with a mound of clay which she has been working into a rough version of the same piece. She is wiping her hands.

'Your cousin,' says Mr Brodie, who will not know the ins and outs of our family, 'is learning how to model. And she is proving to be a very good pupil.'

Which is all well and good, but there is something in Cousin Amelia's intentness that makes me doubt she is going to have the time to do this sculpting as well as being the company for my father we had hoped.

And so it is not such a surprise when I hear Uncle Noel and Dada talking about Cousin Amelia's trip to Italy where she will study the great sculptors of Greece and Rome and Renaissance Italy.

When I ask Dada if he will miss her, he says we all will, but we have plenty of other company and it is important for Amelia to do the thing she wants when she has the chance. This was his advice when she asked for it on the day of the picnic and I see how I have got things nearly right but also quite wrong.

When Jessie comes to call with Isobel Balfour, Dada tells Isobel he will not make her calotype and if she wants a picture she should go to Mr Howie in Princes Street who is skilled in all the new processes. While they talk, I tell Jessie about my plan for Dada and Cousin Amelia and how it was thwarted. Jessie says my father has never been one to have things mapped out for him and so it might be best if I think about my future rather than his.

So there is nothing I can do, except find my place in the book I put down all those weeks ago. I'm thinking, if Cousin Amelia should fall in love with the blue skies of Italy, maybe I will get to go and see them too.

CHAPTER FOURTEEN

A Litany of Stone

Carrara, Italy, 1858

It was late afternoon and the sun was slipping low through the narrow window of the Academia di Arte in Carrara: too early to walk away from his father's desk, too late to feel any enthusiasm for the work left lying there. Giacomo pushed back his chair and straightened his creaking spine. The twelve months since his accident felt like ten years.

From the window, he watched the baker's boy loping along the pavement and pushed open the casement.

'Hey, Lorenzo, has the coach arrived?'

'I don't think so! Probably held up in Lucca.'

He returned to the desk, both irritated and relieved that Signora Paton wouldn't come calling today. The letter from her patron in the Scottish capital, floating lazily on top of a stack of correspondence, had already acquired a film of the ever-present white dust which he sent shimmering away with a practiced flick of the wrist.

Women visitors were always a puzzle: some flashed invitations with their eyes but if Giacomo responded, and in the past he often had, most scuttled away, shocked at their own forwardness. A few made it easy for him to find his way to their chamber and drew back the bed-sheet in welcome. He sighed at these memories. Women liked a tightly sinewed arm. The pallid skin of an administrator, an administrator with a pronounced limp, did not draw the eye, which was perhaps for the best. He'd begun to tire of the brief dalliances, though not of the work that led to them, the shaping of the stone, the demonstration of its qualities, the brushing of the hand across the bulk of a new slab.

An hour had passed when the knock came at his door. He expected the concierge, clanking his keys, grumbling and chasing him home to his father's empty house but it was a woman, standing against the light, a compact figure, plainly dressed. She came forward, bearing a letter in her outstretched hand.

'*Sono arrivato di Firenze*. Amelia Paton.'

Giacomo rose too quickly and winced at the intensity of the spasm in his leg. His visitor gave no sign of noticing and he breathed deeply to compose himself.

'I am Giacomo Buonarotti. My father has left me in charge.

Still she did not smile. 'Signor Brodie . . . *a scritto?*'

He guessed her Italian was limited. He was pleased to be able to put his hand on the letter he had been reading earlier. 'Welcome to Carrara, Signora. Look, a matching pair. They have found each other!'

His small joke drew no reaction and he felt compelled to continue. 'You travel alone?'

Amelia Paton nodded. The question was hardly necessary. All he could do was to think of another, wishing he had practised his English before her arrival.

'Your accommodation is comfortable?'

She said that everything was in order. To free himself from the torture of further conversation, he offered to escort her back to her pensione.

The route to the Via Ghibelina took them past the marble Duomo where in answer to his invitation Signora Paton said

157

Yes, she would like to go inside. She admired the basilica but didn't genuflect in front of the altar. Her family, she said, did not hold with the Catholic faith, in fact they espoused no organised religion, although the Pieta in Rome had moved her almost to tears.

He was stung by curiosity, something he hadn't felt in a long time, 'You are moved by something you don't believe in?'

'I appreciate any art that comes from conviction, even if I don't share it.'

'And you think there is no God?

'I am sceptical of the trappings of religion, that's not the same. What about you? Do you believe?'

'I am not without doubts.'

Had God deserted him when the mountain fell on his back? That was to presuppose God's interest in him in the first place.

Outside he asked her what she thought of the grotesques leering down on them from the corners of the roof.

'Art allows faith and superstition to co-exist,' she said.

The square was bisected by shadow. She looked up at the circle of the mountain. 'You've had snow already?'

He explained that the white pockmarks were made by quarrying. Snow might come later.

'Of course,' she said, reprimanding herself with a frown.

He admired the energy with which she was pacing the piazza. Most visitors arriving so late would have retired and rung for tea. She was confident but still a stranger and alone.

'Signora Paton. Can I suggest that after you have dined you retire early rather than walk in the town?'

Her shoulders had softened into relaxation. 'Carrara does not strike me as threatening.'

'I hope it is not. However, there are hundreds of quarries worked by thousands of men and lately some . . . factions have taken to congregating in the town to air their grievances. They can become . . .'

'Rowdy?'

'Yes, possibly rowdy.'

'And are those grievances justified?'

It was his job to be aware of such things, not make judgments. 'In some cases, I expect.'

She nodded. 'Where I come from, there is always some discontent.'

'In *Edin-burga*?'

She corrected his pronunciation. 'Edinburgh. My home is a weaving town. When I was a girl, there was often trouble.'

She was alive to his warnings yet there was a composure to Signora Paton. When he wished her good night she gave him her hand which was small and firm.

Most women aspiring to sculpture found the discipline more taxing than they had realised or the obstacles to progress too great. This Scottish woman had a determination which led him to believe she might be different.

His father had found someone willing to take Signora Paton as a pupil and for several days he saw her only through the door of a private studio, clad in a heavy smock. On another day he found her in the public gallery examining paintings with her strangely business-like demeanour. She turned when he entered the room.

'How are you finding Carrara?'

As ever her expression was serious. 'Thank you. I like it a great deal. Except I cannot sleep.'

'Ah, the quarries. People grow accustomed.' He found it hard to sleep without the growl of blasting from the mountain. 'But otherwise are you benefitting from being here?'

'I am broadening my mind. Signor Franelli is teaching me to use plaster rather than wax. Then we'll look at how models are translated into stone.'

He understood *translated*. Materials each had their own language. He noticed her slight frown.

'I can't see how I will ever work at it myself.'

'You don't need to. We have people.'

She nodded. 'I understand I could send a model here to be copied but somehow,' she looked at her hands, 'I would like to feel the rock take shape, to make it come alive myself.'

Since the day when the slab at Pulchratudine had pinned him to the ground, he had been back to the quarries only on the briefest of errands. Students often lacked such curiosity or could easily be dissuaded. Maybe it was time to show the place some forgiveness.

'Would you like to see our marble mountain for yourself? Close up I mean. You would know then where everything comes from.'

When she cared about something her eyes glinted with amber. 'Is it allowed?'

'Not to everyone, but if you have a few hours to spare, I can take you myself.'

He led her out of the building towards the Piazza Gramsci and a line of open carriages. He looked for a driver he recognised and asked to be taken to Fantascritti – with care. There would be a lady on board.

At the edge of the town they bumped off the paved road onto the mountain track, although even here it was even, worn smooth by the wagons that brought the marble down from its lair. The herbs along the verge had lost their summer pungency but still gave fragrance to the air.

She pulled at the rug he insisted she used to protect her clothes from dust. 'You haven't followed in the footsteps of your namesake, Mr Buonarotti. Are you connected to the great Michelangelo?'

Before his spine had become crooked, when he was still bedding students, he had seen the widening of girls' eyes at his name. Amelia Paton asked her question without a trace of coyness.

'Only distantly. And I have never been a sculptor. I was apprenticed as a stonemason until I suffered an injury to my back.'

His accident and its outcome was known to the whole of Carrara. Only Amelia Paton would think he'd been born with a limp and a curve in his spine.

'You had to change your occupation. That can't have been easy.'

He shook his head. 'We never know what lies ahead of us. I am grateful to still be alive.' Was he grateful for a life that had changed entirely? Until now he had simply accepted it.

He explained how the blasting was a two-edged sword. 'As well as loosening the slabs, it causes them to . . .' He let his hands fly upwards and apart.

'Disintegrate?'

'Yes, disintegrate.' He liked the precision with which she used words. 'You are expanding my vocabulary, Miss Paton.'

'Amelia. Call me Amelia.'

There was no suggestion of intimacy. Her eyes were on the quarries just coming into view, her fingers hooked around the edge of the carriage.

'Very well, Amelia.'

Perhaps it was his pronunciation, but she seemed unsettled by his use of the name she had suggested.

The driver urged the pony up the track as far as the main entrance to Fantascritti. Giacomo pointed out where some seams were blurred at the edges with a new growth of vegetation while others, higher up, were bleakly white. 'They must go higher all the time,' he said.

He helped her down from the trap, spoke briefly to the foreman and led her up the main path used by quarrymen, explaining how each variation of the marble had its admirers.

'Every stone carries the landscape within it, don't you think?' she said.

'Is there no stone in Scotland that can be used for sculpture?'

'I don't think grey granite would ever yield to a sculptor's hammer.'

He was pleased to have drawn a smile from her.

Back in the main concourse he was hailed by a group of masons slumped against newly harvested slabs of travertine. He introduced Amelia as 'Artista Scozesa' and she asked questions which he put to them on her behalf.

He saw her attentiveness wear down their suspicion. Only his old friend Massimo nudged him as he passed and muttered about his *nuova ragazza*. As she walked away to admire the view and the men heaved themselves up to go back to work, he walked around the yard, running his hand over blocks in different stages of preparation, feeling the grain in the rock, closing his eyes to let each stone speak. He still heard their voices. He was lame but not deaf.

A wagon drew alongside, pulled by a mule. Its load of dressed stone was in the charge of a relative by marriage. His face was set in leather creases, teeth yellow with tobacco he had somehow acquired from a merchant on the coast. His mutilated arm was tied inside the sleeve of a cotton jacket.

'Giacomo, what are you doing up here, you madman?'

'I could ask you the same, Sandro.'

'Some of us have to work for a living.'

Giacomo clapped him on the back, feeling the shoulder blades, clothed in too little flesh.

Amelia had come back and was watching. He led her back to the carriage. She rubbed her hand over her eyes, leaving a grey smirch on her cheek.

'You are tired. I've kept you too long.'

She shook her head. 'I should be thankful I'm not as tired as the mule driver.'

'Sandro lost a hand when a fuse was lit in error. Driving the mules is all he can do.'

'This mountain takes its toll.'

'Only when men disturb it.'

He left her at the door of the pensione.

'Giacomo. If you are free any evening, I would enjoy your

162

company over dinner. Even after a hard day the evenings can be . . . dull.'

So she had been asking about him. *Where does he live? Does he have a wife?* In anyone else, such discreet enquiries would have been a cause for amusement. He concealed a smile. Amelia Paton did not make meaningless advances. In all likelihood she didn't make advances of any kind. He could take her offer at face value.

He bowed. 'Thank you. An evening in your company would be most welcome.'

'I'll ask my landlady if she can cook for an extra visitor tomorrow. We eat at six.'

After dinner the other guests left them alone. He found her accent surprisingly easy to follow and his English was coming back to him.

'So what is your interest, Amelia? Portrait busts? Or larger pieces?'

'My interest is in character, regardless of the shape or form of the statue. If someone is to live forever, we must convey their true self.'

'And the qualities that make them worthy of eternal life?'

'Yes, of course, although a subject needn't have attained greatness to be interesting, or beautiful.'

He considered his plate of veal, wondering if he wanted to continue this discussion. 'So is there beauty in all of us? In the driver with his missing hand?' *In me*, he could have said but didn't want to make her uncomfortable.

Outside a group of boys could be heard on the corner of the next alley, slapping cards on to a barrel top, one accusing the other of cheating. She found her voice and he brought his attention back to her face, impassive as it so often was.

'Grace is maybe a better word. Grace of spirit can be found in all kinds of people and places.'

'But in sculpture we celebrate the body.'

163

'I disagree. We work in the physical form but the body is only one of its representations.'

She was deliberately obfuscating and he shook his head involuntarily.

'I've upset you?' she said.

He let it go. 'No. Don't worry.'

Somehow she divined the source of his discomfort. 'How badly damaged is your back?'

'The bones have healed but are misaligned. They create pressures in other places.'

'There's no treatment?'

'Nothing a surgeon can do. There is a risk of total paralysis.'

At the end of the meal she rose and wished him goodnight. Without deliberation, he leaned over her hand. 'Thank you for your most entertaining company.'

The expression was conventional. She stepped away from him with a smile. 'I'm not sure I am the one to provide entertainment,' she said, 'but I've enjoyed our talk a great deal. Good night, Giacomo.'

On an impulse he took her hand back and kissed it. Her fingers, pressed so suddenly to his lips, fluttered in surprise but she did not draw her hand away.

After two more dinners, by which time they knew each other's thoughts on most topics in art, geology and religion, she gave herself to him with the same quiet determination with which he had seen her approach everything.

'You are . . . untouched,' he said afterwards.

She smoothed away his frown. 'Not any more.'

He ran his hand along the length of her, from ankle to waist to collar-bone. The trip to the mountain had made him hungry, not just for a woman. 'Parian marble,' he said, as he stroked her white calf.

She flexed her small square foot against his hand. 'And what would you know of Parian?'

Even her teasing had a serious edge. 'I have seen it. In Athens and Rome.'

'And touched it?'

'I work with stone. I always touch.'

She let him complete his litany: in the veins of her thigh he found the blue-green of Arabescato; in her forearm, freckled by the sun, a streak of Calacatta gold.

What about Michelangelo, she wanted to know. Did she have any of the famous *Statuaria* in her?

He would not compare her to the Pieta or even some Roman deity. If by lying with him she was giving herself to some other Buonarotti he did not mind. Perhaps it was his birthright.

In the nights, the crack and boom of the gunpowder brought her to shuddering wakefulness. When they made love, he pictured the slabs shearing off and lying silent on the quarry floor, like books, waiting to be read.

It was some days before he asked her. Why me? Why now?'

'My father likes to quote Ecclesiastes.'

'I thought he didn't hold with religion?'

'He knows his Bible. *To everything there is a season. To sow, to learn, to embrace all that is given.* This is my time to know a man, to know you.'

As to the sowing, they were careful. She did not intend to go home with a child inside her.

She liked to work her fingers down his back, probing its irregularities, soothing and arousing, sometimes finding the spot that made him arch and cry out.

She stroked away the pain. 'You should see a bonesetter,' she said.

The man in Pisa made Giacomo stand naked in front of him. The room was barely warmed by a mean fire and a full human skeleton, its whitened bones joined with twine, added a macabre glow to the farthest corner.

The bone-setter said he had seen worse. That didn't mean he could cure him.

'But you can try?'

He wiped his hands on a rag that smelled of almond oil. 'It will take a while. And it will hurt.'

The treatments were a week apart. The pummeling was less painful than he expected. Something in the skeleton's slack-jawed rictus told him this might be a deception, that worse was to come. He began to associate the smell of almond oil with a mute apprehension which gripped him at the start of every visit, gradually dissipating in the rhythm of the man's hands, lulling him to a dream-like state in which Amelia floated next to him. The bone-setter sensed his fear. 'Be calm,' he said, 'and the treatment will be more beneficial. We will get to the manipulation more quickly.'

If it hadn't been for the outlay of money, Giacomo might have told him to continue with the loosening of sinew and muscle, to forget the wrenching of bone that would bring it to an end.

One night, as the quarries roared, he asked Amelia why she had chosen sculpture. Had she read of Properzia de' Rossi and her peach kernels? There were no peach stones in Scotland, she said, but all her life she had liked the feel of things and as a *bairn*, a *bambina*, she had made models in wax to pass the time.

When he said there had been women before, she said more would come, she was sure of it, as time went on. He imagined her encouraging other Scottish *signore*. 'And will you send them to me?' he asked. 'For their education?'

It was a joke. He saw too late how it assumed her departure from Carrara.

She raised herself on one elbow to look him straight in the eye. A hank of hair fell over her shoulder, lustrous in the moonlight.

'Maybe I will,' she said. 'You're a good teacher.'

And so her leaving was agreed, although he had never meant it to be.

He put his face against the curtain of hair and spoke into her breast. 'Have I taken advantage of my position?'

She eased her nipple to his mouth and wound her legs around him. 'No more,' she said, 'than I have taken advantage of mine.'

In Pisa, the pummeling grew more intense. He thought of Amelia's fingertips and how pain and pleasure were not so distant from each other. The bonesetter said the manipulation might take several attempts. He should plan to stay for three days. On the second day, the man whispered in his ear. 'Think of the woman, my son.'

Giacomo tried to take himself to the darkness of the pensione but the smell of almonds was distracting. He could only yield to what was coming, fall into the skeleton's empty eyes. When the rock had fallen, he had felt only numb. This pain was how it should have been.

She was too angry to notice how much straighter he was standing. 'Where have you been?'

'Looking to my future, the future you don't want to share.'

She recoiled from him, eyebrows arched. 'You never asked me to share it. Anyway I can't stay here. What would I do?'

She had a letter from her brother. His wife was with child.

'You're not a midwife.'

'But I should be there,' she said.

'Why don't you stay? Make your models and see them cast in stone. What will you do in Scotland except find a husband, have a Scottish child?'

She laughed and shook her head. 'The time for that is past. I have other things to do.'

He stretched tall in front of her, reaching his hands above

his head like a diver. 'I thought you were looking for beauty and for truth. Which stone will you choose for me?'

Seeing him made whole, she covered her mouth with her hand. But even so, he knew it would not change her mind.

On the day she was due to leave there was trouble amongst the workers at Pulchratudine and he wanted to see the latest stones, how they compared with the older workings.

Arriving at the quarry, he pictured her thanking his father who had returned to his place in the Academia, telling him how she would always remember Carrara, the mountains and the marble. He liked to think she would remember the details, the dust of the studio, the noise of the quarries, the stubborn knots in his back.

On his way back he met the driver with the withered hand.

'Always some trouble up here,' Giacomo said.

'Men are easier to deal with than women,' Sandro replied.

His affair with Amelia was more widely known than he'd realised. 'You may be right,' he said. 'But the least trouble of all is the stone we pull from the mountain. We can shape it as we like, or cast it aside and start again. I've never heard it complain.'

Sandro's laugh was harsh from inhaling marble dust and roadside rubble. 'We'll be seeing more of you up here, then?'

'Maybe. Or it might be time for me to get away from this sullen valley.'

'You're going to *Edimburga?*'

A buzzard wheeled and dived on some creature scuttling in a tussock of rosemary. Giacomo bent down and picked up a one of the countless chips of marble and blew off the dust to reveal cream laced with brown. He put it in his pocket, for luck.

'No. I hear the Scottish cities are grey. I might go to Calabria, or Greece. Wherever the marble is pure and white.'

CHAPTER FIFTEEN

Open to Interpretation

Mary Gowans, Edinburgh, 1861

James was away on business and I was staying a day or two at my father's house in Edinburgh when Amelia Paton sent a note to say she would call. She had been back from Italy for more than a year, during which time I had married and become Mary Gowans instead of Mary Brodie. Since moving to Merchiston, I'd lost touch for a while with my friend and fellow sculptress.

It was January, damp but mild, and I had a cold brought on by the unseasonable weather and my return to the sooty streets of the city. I snivelled into a hankie as I waited for her to arrive, but my spirits were good. My father's house was a step back into my previous life, less luxurious than my new home but free of the wings of rumour that beat about the chimney stacks of Rockville. The thought of Amelia's company tempted me to think that my old life might still be reclaimed, at least in part.

When she came in, her quiet smile revived me even more and I knew from the warmth of her embrace that there would be no awkwardness between us despite the lapse of time.

'You must come out to the house,' I told her, knowing that her visit would spur me on and send me back to my studio where a number of sculptures lay unfinished.

'I will,' she said, 'and it's high time I met James.'

James' character does not always win him friends, so the folk who visit do so mainly to see not him but the interior of his most famous creation. Amelia, of course, was not of that ilk and the twinkle in her eye told me she was either innocent of the gossip flying around or had discounted it entirely.

Mother brought in some tea and the three of us sat for a while, talking of Amelia's travels and how she was staying with her brother, Noel Paton, in his fine new house in George Square. I spoke of James' plans to have father's sculptures in the garden at Rockville and got down some new books to show Amelia. When Mother left us, I asked about her work.

'Sharing a studio hasn't been easy. I am always under my brother's feet, or he under mine.' She laid down her cup with a certain deliberation. 'But not for much longer.'

I waited for the news she had apparently been keeping until we were alone.

'I'm to be married.'

I set down my tea-cup so hard the spoon clattered from the saucer and fell to the floor.

Although she has always felt more like a sister, Amelia is nearly as old as my mother and has a fierce independence of spirit. I had never thought of her as some man's wife. By the time I retrieved the spoon, I'd recovered my composure and asked who the husband was to be.

'Who do you think?"

'Don't tease me!' I replied, but she was determined to keep me guessing.

'I'll give you a clue. He is a widower, like your James.'

There is no widower quite like James but I put my mind to solving the puzzle. Amelia was well set up with her brother. There must be some advantage to her or her family in the impending marriage. Then it came to me. Noel Paton was hand-in-glove with the man who had so often walked into our sculpture class and nodded to Amelia as he passed. 'A family friend' she had called him. It was so long since his wife had died I had forgotten he was a widower.

'Mr Hill?'

She nodded. Amelia had always had talent and wasn't afraid of hard work, yet what more could a woman on the edge of an artistic career ask than to have the Secretary of the Scottish Academy at her back? 'He will surely set you on your way.'

'I hope so, but keep it to yourself. He and I haven't had the chance to talk since it was decided.'

So the family was behind it. All the same, there were worse matches to be made. I pictured him striding along Princes Street, acknowledging greetings from all and sundry. 'He is still handsome . . . for his years.'

She gave me a stern look, as if romance was the last thing on her mind. 'He is sixty and a man like any other, usually gracious, ill-tempered if something displeases him.'

There was a twinkle in her eye for all that. 'So when will it be?'

'I don't know, because he'll see his daughter married first.'

Then we came to her real interest.

'Did you ever meet the first Mrs Gowans?' she asked me.

From habit I drew back in my seat at the mention of Elizabeth but reminded myself Amelia was thinking of her own situation, not mine. I shook my head.

'Were you a friend of James while she was alive?'

It was a story I rarely told. Amelia, though, was somebody I felt could hear it. 'I'd met him just the once. Faither introduced us at a talk in the Calton Rooms. He was already well-known and I asked if there was any of his work in Edinburgh. He mentioned some terraces and the cottages where he lived with his wife. Practical and useful he called them, but said his best was still to come. He had a way of rocking back and forth as he spoke. Something in that rocking drew me towards him and made me feel I would be part of this future he was planning.'

Amelia listened, her head cocked, without offering a response.

171

'Elizabeth died not long after, and within a month James was in my father's study, asking for my hand.'

Here Amelia raised her eyebrows. 'There was a connection between your families?'

I shook my head. 'James was already well-off. He owns the stone quarries, you know, but faither didn't insist. I was young and bonny, he said. If James didn't suit me there would be somebody else, sooner or later.'

'But James did suit you.' She was looking at me with new interest, acknowledging James and I had married for something other than convenience.

'Of course he is older than me and less . . . personable than your intended.' Amelia shifted in her chair as if she had forgotten for the minute she was about to be Mrs Hill. 'But I remembered that first meeting and how I had sensed a closeness between us. I didn't hesitate.'

'Some men have a kind of magnetism,' she said, 'a force of personality, I suppose.'

I studied the ring he had given me on our wedding. 'Some call it love,' I said, 'but I have never known what to call it.'

We allowed ourselves a minute to contemplate such things.

'You fell under his spell,' she said. 'It has never happened to me, not really.'

I was surprised by the wistful look in her eye. While she thought herself unlucky not to have felt this uncontrollable attraction, I wondered if I would ever escape from the spell James had laid on me.

After she went home to her brother's house, I pictured Amelia telling her sister-in-law about our meeting and how, sooner or later, as they walked together over the Meadows, Margaret Paton would let slip that James Gowans, the famous architect, had done away with his wife.

When Amelia came to Rockville, my head had cleared. I showed her my studio and the armature I had begun for a new figure of Cupid. Then we sat in the morning room overlooking the garden. March was colder than January. A frost had fallen overnight and the advancing sun had made the lawn into two triangles, one green, one white. My father's marble figures peeped from between the trees just as James had planned. Amelia said what a fine backdrop the garden made for the statues although Pan, in his nakedness, might worry about the effect of the cold on his manhood. How like Amelia this was. In the sculpture class we had often laughed into our sleeves as my father, unaccustomed to the presence of ladies, danced around the topic of male anatomy. Here at least we could laugh openly and for a while I forgot the shadow I lived under.

She told me her bust of Miranda was on show in Glasgow. She and her brother were going to view it that weekend.

'Just wait until you are Mrs Hill,' I told her. 'The Edinburgh Academy will have to show it then.'

She shook her head, not in denial but as if the thought was a bother to her, like a wasp that wouldn't be waved away. 'I know he'll help, though I hope I can win more commissions on my own merits.'

I saw she was warming to the idea of the marriage which was to be in November. Her only uncertainties were about the house. 'His sister Mary and her family will still be with us. He's giving me the old calotype workshop.'

She looked around our high-ceilinged morning room and the contortions of the plaster frieze. 'What I would give for a new place, just to ourselves.'

She stopped herself, maybe recalling there was a price to be paid for such luxury, a price she didn't like to mention.

To rescue her from her sudden silence, I said, 'James will be home for his dinner. Would you like me to show you the rest of the house before he gets here?'

I took her to the kitchens and the Jacobean dining room, then up the Japanese staircase. She exclaimed at the convenience of the gas lighting and the heavy embossed wallpaper. We stepped out on the balcony of the pagoda tower where our breathing was nearly stopped by the cold and we kept our hands inside our sleeves. The city lay before us from the Pentlands to Princes Street.

'All of Edinburgh would like to see this,' she said. 'You could charge a penny a time.' She put her hand to her mouth in embarrassment but her words still wound away into the blueness of the sky.

It was my turn to pretend nothing was amiss. 'Luckily we have no need of pennies,' I said, 'though I could sometimes do with the company.'

On the way down, her hand smoothed the turned mahogany stair rail and she let her fingertips brush the silk-lined curtains. It was time to say what she wouldn't put into words. I showed her the bathroom, where the slanting sun made jewels of the red and turquoise tiles, explaining how the water ran in pipes, already warm.

'I've never seen anything like it,' she said and the silence was broken only by the gurgling of the plumbing and the thrum of secrets.

'Amelia, I know what you've heard, so why don't you speak of it?'

She was studying the exotic border of lemon and bay trees, modeled on the harem of Istanbul. 'Why would I talk about something I know isn't true?'

She had still not met James. Her respect was not for him, but for me and the life I had chosen.

I leaned over the bath to look out of the window where I saw two women stop on their way past and look up, admiring Rockville, talking about its owner. I considered calling down to them that everything was just as they thought so they could stop wondering. It's the lack of knowledge, the possibility of crime, that feeds the flame of rumour.

I sat down on the edge of the bath and shook out my skirt.

'It is better out in the open between us. Elizabeth Gowans was found dead in her bath. And some say James was her killer.'

Amelia was perfectly calm. 'And do you think he had a hand in it?'

I let my petticoat settle and savoured the words. 'I know he didn't.'

Her expression didn't change and I was flooded with relief. I should have opened the window after all and let the truth fly naked over Edinburgh. 'He was undone by her death but he kept his grief to himself.'

'As most men do,' she said, and there was a softening in her voice. She took my elbow, raised me from my awkward seat then put her arms around me. 'Folk are cruel. I'm so sorry you have to put up with this.'

We left the bathroom and made our way down the staircase.

'So how did she die? Did he tell you?'

'They don't know for sure. It was only after our marriage was announced that the accusations began. And then there was Rockville.'

'Because he built it for you.'

I looked up the stairwell but the top landing was in shadow. No means of escape had appeared.

'That's what James has always said. Those who don't revile me envy me, the princess in her own castle.'

'But that hardly means he killed his wife.'

Amelia is never other than sensible.

James joined us for our dinner which was served by the housekeeper, the maid having gone home because of some petty dissatisfaction. He and Amelia were polite to each other, too polite. I watched her study him when his attention was elsewhere – on his mutton pie or while talking to me about the maid of whom he said it was her loss rather than ours.

Amelia was trying to like my husband but she was finding it hard. His looks are not of the classic style and some women can't see past a balding head or a sharp nose. More likely the quality in James that attracted me had the opposite effect on her – I have seen this in others, men and women. I guessed James was not drawn to her either but he put on his best smile and asked what she made of the house.

Her discomfort made her praise too fulsome. 'Rockville has given you the chance to try out new styles,' she said, 'and show how they can work.'

He was more than satisfied at this perception from a fellow artist. 'Tell your friends,' he said. 'An architect's career depends on good opinion, especially from one such as you.'

We talked of Amelia's marriage. 'A fine man indeed,' James said over his plum duff. 'I have never heard anybody speak ill of him. You must bring him here when you are wed . . . or before even.' He wanted D.O. Hill on his side. I sometimes wished his ambition was less obvious.

After the meal, James took the carriage to do some business in the town and Amelia waited for her own trap to arrive. We sat again in the morning room where the lawn had darkened to a green sward. I apologised for James's eagerness but she said ambition was no bad thing and that she cared only that I was happy, which she could see that I was. I was pleased to have done a good job on that score.

'Your garden has a high wall,' she said. 'Rumours stop on the road outside.'

That is when I could have told her what James said when he first brought me here. 'This house and you in it has made me famous. Let them speak all they like, as long as they know the name of James Gowans.'

Even now he could put a stop to the rumour any time he likes but prefers to keep folk guessing, to leave things, as he calls it, open to interpretation. And I am expected to do the same. I wanted to tell Amelia this if only to feel less alone but my loyalty is to him and Amelia is the one who said I was under his spell.

We chose the Chinese bedroom, even though the sheets would have to be changed. When he had taken me, we lay undisturbed. He has a way of divining my thoughts. 'Your Miss Paton will do well. Hill has influence all over the country. Get him here as soon as you can.'

He was naked but he likes me to stay clothed. His hands began to voyage under my nightgown. One foray is rarely enough for either of us.

'I told Amelia the truth about Elizabeth.'

This stopped his marauding, which I realised had been my purpose. It was the first time I had felt this need for separation.

He sat up, leaning on his elbow, and smiled down at me. 'Good for you. The more times we tell the truth, the fewer believe it.'

'She believes it.'

The rough beginnings of his beard brushed my cheek. 'That's all right,' he said. 'There will be plenty more that don't and they will talk to all and sundry about the man who built a pagoda after killing his wife.'

This is his perverse way of paying them back, the gossip-mongers. He claims it has got him attention as far afield as Inverness.

'Do you not think about her?'

He doesn't like it when I mention Elizabeth. He got up from the bed and began to dress himself. 'You know we can't help rumour so we may as well turn it to our own good.' He stopped in the act of putting on his shoes. 'It doesn't bother you, does it?'

What would have been the point of saying Yes?

I've seen Amelia only once since then. All was well between her and David, she said. I had never heard the artist called by his first name and said without thinking, 'David, now?'

Her skin tends to sallowness but I detected the start of a blush. 'I told him that if we're to share a bed, I can hardly call him by his initials.'

We shared a smile. Amelia may not be under anybody's spell but she deserves some pleasure with her widower.

Soon they'll be married and I'll invite the both of them but before that she can come alone and I will show her the original plans for Rockville, dated six months before Elizabeth died. It was to be her house, not mine. I'll tell her how James likes to play his games. They won't last forever and with Amelia beside me, I will find them easier to bear.

I sometimes picture her in the grey house on the hill and remember she is envying me and James our isolation. I thought of her only yesterday as I lay in the bath. James was waiting for me in the Chinese bedroom whose sheets are laundered, sometimes daily, by the new maid. I lay there longer than usual, the water cooling, studying the patterns on the tiles, checking the door was locked and remembering how the Turks are said to have a cruel streak.

THE CALOTYPE
RECONSIDERED

CHAPTER SIXTEEN

A Day of Ghosts

London, January 1863

Elizabeth Eastlake got up from her writing desk to close the casement, shutting out the clamour of hawkers on Fitzroy Square. She had an article to write and two books on modern art awaiting review. Unusually, since Charles was Director of the National Gallery, no invitations had been given or received. She looked forward to a busy day with these and some small maters of domestic management followed by a tranquil evening. When Charles came home, they would have supper together and plan which European cities they would visit next year in search of treasures. What better way to fill a dark winter's night?

But first there was the post, only two items, brought in earlier by the butler and left on her favourite writing table. Although this dearth of communication was a matter of some relief, it made the missives that had arrived all the more interesting. The first, a packet, probably a magazine or proof article, contained the promise of more work to be done and was the less intriguing of the two.

The other, a plain letter, bore an Edinburgh postmark, something immediately in its favour. She was overcome by a wave of nostalgia for the gracious crescents and wind-racked skies of the north. The hand in which the envelope was addressed did not belong to any of her usual correspondents from Auld Reekie. She could have simply slit the seal and unmasked the writer but there was something of the detective in her and instead she went to the bureau and rifled in one of its smaller drawers until she found what she was looking for, an old calotype print – how the softness of its tones still appealed – foxed at the edges but still clear, of her younger self. Turning it over, she found the handwritten inscription, *Elizabeth Rigby, 1844.* Nearly twenty years ago! With the letter still in her other hand, she compared the small and hurried script on each and concluded what she had suspected all along. The photographer and the letter-writer were one and the same, her old friend, D.O. Hill.

The frisson of pleasure this brought was only slightly muted by the realisation that that these were the first words to have passed between them since she had left Edinburgh. Not that there was any reason that her marriage and the move to London should have ended her friendship with the Scottish artist, nor had there been any rift, any real rift, between them at the time of her departure. Since then, circumstances, she assured herself, had simply not brought them together. D.O. was not a great traveler beyond the bounds of his bonny Scotland and her trips North had not required a visit to Rock House.

She let out an involuntary sigh. If meetings couldn't be arranged, there was always the happy consolation of correspondence. Since there had been none between them, she was forced to admit this friendship had simply slipped into disuse. But the moment of melancholy was easy to shake off when its cure lay in her hand. She looked forward to having that dear familiar voice – in writing or in person – mingling in the stream of friends and acquaintances who made up her social round.

How she would enjoy showing the letter to Charles. In fact she would make a point of reading it in his company, just in case he imagined any lingering intimacy between her and D.O., recently married, she now recalled, to a sculptress.

Charles, she was sure, would welcome a more personal contact with the Secretary to the Scottish Academy. Surely an invitation to London would be issued and the new Mrs Hill would make up the company perfectly. And what of the daughter? She did some calculations as to the girl's age. Charlotte might also enjoy a trip to see the London fashions, in which case Elizabeth could fetch up a few nieces or younger acquaintances to keep her company.

The chime of the Louis XIV clock brought her back from exploring a dozen streams and tributaries of possibility emanating from the letter, including the invitation list for when the Hills would come to dine at Fitzroy Square.

But she had work to do. The irritation of the larger and less amiable packet had been more than counterbalanced by the joy residing in its fellow envelope and she opened the weightier of the two with something like alacrity, extracting a sheaf of printed sheets entitled: "On the deficiencies of Lady Eastlakes's review of *Jane Eyre*, a re-examination of Charlotte Bronte for the modern woman" by Harriet E. Blenkinsop.

Elizabeth could not have been more offended if the letter had contained a black spider or hissing serpent and immediately stood up as if to be out of its predatory path. She expelled the air from her lungs in a grunt of indignation that would have cleared the sheets from the desk had they been of lighter quality. Since the paper was heavy enough to resist her antagonism, she picked the sheets up gingerly and strode with them to the window, intending to hurl them out, either to land on the smoking brazier kept by a hunched workman on the corner of the square or to be blown directly to the grimy Thames where they might turn to sludge. However, by the time she had wrestled with the window latch, her more usual temperance had returned and she simply held the offending article at arm's length.

'Will I never be free of you?' she exclaimed, wondering if

she was addressing Miss Blenkinsop (of whom she had never heard), Miss Bronte (God rest her soul) or her old self, Elizabeth Rigby, since it was she who had caused the original commotion.

This venting of anger did something to soothe her, but also brought the maid running in. 'Is something amiss, Ma'am?'

'No more than usual, Hetty. But could I ask you for a glass of water? I'm feeling a little flushed.'

As the maid bobbed out, Elizabeth picked up a note that had slipped from the envelope.

Dear Lady Eastlake,
Before publishing this proof I thought you might like to formulate a reply which we would be happy to publish in the same issue. A chance to lay this particular ghost to rest?
Wm McPherson

She viewed the florid script with some distaste. As the new editor of the *Review*, McPherson had failed so far to endear himself. She wondered why he was giving the upstart Miss Blenkinsop (for Elizabeth would have known her if she had any literary standing) and her thoughts on Bronte such attention when there were so many other interesting books to discuss. When Hetty brought the water she ordered coffee to follow and considered how this was turning out to be a day of ghosts.

At noon, Sir Charles came home unexpectedly. Luncheon together was a rare treat and the dear man saw her distemper straight away, laying his hand on hers. 'My dear, what on earth has happened to upset you?'

She explained, trying to make light of this new impertinence. 'My review is more than ten years old. Why is it still dragged up for examination?'

'Would you rather it were forgotten?'

Trust Charles to find the nub of it. No writer wanted oblivion. 'It's only that I am constantly . . . *misconstrued*.'

His smile verged on the mischievous. 'You certainly showed no love for Miss Eyre.'

His fine hands poised over the cutlery reminded her of his visits to Edinburgh, when he had dined with them so many times before coming forward with his proposal. She had been patient, her mind flitting all the while between her respect for Eastlake and the depth of her feelings for D.O. 'Jane is a very unattractive character and Rochester an absolute brute. These facts will never change.'

Charles digested this along with his baked haddock. 'Maybe you would feel differently if you read it again?'

It had never occurred to her to reread the book. Once had been more than enough. On the other hand Charles was right. A book didn't change but its reader sometimes did.

She shook off this possibility. 'I'm sure many people didn't read the whole review, only those gobbets that have been extracted and quoted so freely. It angers me that I was said to have taken against women when in the larger part of it I called for better treatment for our poor governesses.'

Charles was silent. How patiently he dealt with such waves of invective, allowing them to break over him and diminish to a mere swell. That was because he loved her. She indulged herself with a question to which she knew what his answer would be.

'Do I seem unwomanly to you?'

He got up and put his arm around her shoulder. It was a novelty to have him looming over her and she leaned her face against his frock coat. 'No woman could be more intelligent, forthright or beautiful,' he said. 'Have I not told you that before?'

He could not conceal a look at his pocket watch and so she let him go.

Returning to her drawing room, she decided the letter from D.O. was best left for later when her passions would be less aroused. Instead, she would read the tawdry article, send her response and free herself from her lingering irritation. Yet the French clock went through an hour of chimes without a word being written. The ghosts of D.O. Hill and Jane Eyre continued to stalk the room.

How kind Charles had been when they first met in London, how doggedly he had pursued her back and forth. Barely ten years younger than the century, she would have been foolish to turn down the rational happiness he offered and there had never been a moment in the intervening years when she had not felt bathed in the light of his true affection. Yet, when his proposal arrived, D.O. still had a hold on her heart. Accepting Charles and leaving Edinburgh also meant leaving him.

Then Miss Eyre came along with her mean childhood and passionate response to the tempestuous and immoderate Rochester. Had she been harsh on Jane whose choices were in such contrast to her own? There was nothing tempestuous about D.O. Hill – a more gracious man she had never met – but she had dampened down her own passion, fearing that for all his good-natured banter, flirtation even, his feelings for her were not of the same depth. If they had been, would carnal desire (she had to acknowledge its existence at least on her side) have been a sound basis for marriage? She had been no more severe with Jane than she had been with herself.

After her wedding, on a sunlit day in Edinburgh, any doubts she had disappeared like snow in spring. She had become not just Charles' wife but an equal partner in all his interests and activities. She knew it was even murmured that the National Gallery was as much hers as its Director's. This was clearly nonsense but she would never deny her own expertise or refuse to share it. She had never been a woman of hearth and home.

She bit her lip and her fingers strayed to the Bible lying on her desk, tracing the outline of letters on its tooled leather binding. With a child to fill her days, would it have been otherwise? Their tiny daughter, born in the early days of her marriage, had hurried back to the Almighty without taking a single breath. Elizabeth took a deep breath to dispel the threat of tears. She always bowed to the will of God, though the loss of her dear one had been the greatest test of her faith.

She steadied her thoughts and turned back to the words of Blenkinsop who like so many others accused her of betraying her fellow women when nothing could be farther from the truth. Surely she had championed women by the example of her own life? She was the first woman to have been published in the *Review*. And in her work with Charles and in her support of governesses, she had been a standard-bearer for the female sex. Not to mention taking poor Effie under her wing in that dreadful business with Ruskin, an act of female solidarity which had caused even Charles to raise an eyebrow.

With a groan she took up her pen. She would not regret her pronouncements on Miss Bronte's book. Armed with her new confidence, she set about her response, making no apology for her review of *Jane Eyre* and making plain how she had supported women's causes in a way she saw fit in the eyes of God.

Once she had begun, the words flowed unbidden from her hand. Her mind, however, snagged on that memory of motherhood and once more she inhabited the old sadness. Her daughter would now have been ten years old. His daughter was perhaps on the cusp of marriage. She had been only a mite during the Edinburgh years, a pixie of a child who played hide and seek when she and D.O. hoped not to be disturbed. Now she was most likely a tall and lovely girl with her father's bearing and, he had always said, her mother's grey eyes. If things had been different, would Charlotte have been an older friend to her dear one, just as she had been a friend to Effie and so many others? She berated herself for the foolishness of such speculations. At least she had driven away the tearful moment.

By supper time her article was almost finished. Since her musings had resulted in some crossings out and an inky blot caused by an errant tear, she would read it though again the following day and make a fair copy to send to McPherson.

Before dinner, she changed into her blue velvet – it was still too cold for taffeta – and made sure her coiffure, which often grew dishevelled when she was writing with gusto, was repaired.

Charles said she was looking much better.

'I'm feeling better. I have written my response.'

He looked at her over his wine glass. 'Are you sure you want to engage in a new battle?'

'Have you ever known me turn one down?'

Again his hand, the hand of a man of taste and discretion, was on hers. 'I don't like to see you upset.'

It was time to think of happier things. As they waited for the cabinet pudding to arrive, she excused herself and returned, bearing the letter from Edinburgh.

'Look. We have a letter from Mr Hill. I saved it to be sure of a good end to the day.'

Charles' smile had an occasional tightness which made him look plaintive but he peered at the envelope with interest.

'We should invite him here with his new wife. You barely met him in Edinburgh and I feel our families' – she stumbled a little over the word – 'could have much to share.'

Charles nodded a little abstractedly and went to the sideboard where, forgetful of the imminent arrival of pudding, he helped himself to nuts and figs.

'I can't think when we will find the time for visitors this year, but I dare say . . .'

Elizabeth felt a little frustrated at his lack of interest in what would be a significant event in her social calendar.

'Anyway, hadn't you better see what he has to say?'

Of course, the letter was unopened. She blinked and saw how foolish she had been to rattle on without ascertaining D.O.'s news. What strange conjunction of fates had led him to issue an invitation to her after all these years? Had something in particular occurred?

It was only as she took a knife to slit the envelope that she considered the possibility of bad news, only when she saw black-edge to the paper that her breath caught in her throat.

The single page bore a printed announcement of the death of Charlotte Dalgleish, *nee* Hill. *In childbirth* was added in his own hand. *May she and all our bairns rest in peace.*

It was many years since she had wept so freely. Charles murmured his condolences. 'So sad . . . such a young age,' and she knew how disproportionate her anguish must seem. He comforted her and stroked her hair as she told him how D.O. would be more stricken than most by the death of the one constant star in his firmament. 'I never saw a man and daughter so . . . entwined in each other,' was the only way she could describe it. Charles most likely guessed that her other sorrow had returned but knew that to mention it would only give it air to breathe.

She retired to her room and closed the door. There were too many reasons for grief and not all of them could be shared. The letter was still in her hand. *All our bairns.* Despite the lack of correspondence, he had known of her loss, just as she had known of his marriage. She had been right in thinking the thread of affection between them had stretched thin but never broken. How she wished she had known as much in her darkest days. How she wished she was by his side.

Her self-imposed privacy had stolen any need for composure. In front of the looking glass, she undid her greying hair and let it fall around her tear-stained face. She could deceive herself no longer. She had walked away from love for the sake of a comfortable life. She had stood up for women but not for herself. She ripped at the neck of her dress so roughly that the fastenings came off and threw her pearl necklace onto the floor. What use were jewels and velvet in a life so full of sorrow?

Next day she rose late, but was composed. All of this was God's will. She had never before resisted Him in this way and would not do so again. She completed her toilet, chose an old grey dress and took the sparsest of breakfasts before asking Hetty for her coat.

'Is that wise, Ma'am? Sir Charles said you were unwell. And it looks like rain.'

'I am not unwell, thank you, and I have an umbrella. If Sir Charles comes back, tell him I am visiting the cemetery. Don't expect me before luncheon.'

It was a good three miles but on this particular day there was nothing else she needed to do. Along the Marylebone and Harrow roads she paid little attention to what she saw, allowing her long legs to carry her onwards through a fine drizzle which made the air heavy as if with dew. It had a cleansing effect and she breathed evenly in the January light.

Her child had no name but she did have a grave in the plot where she and Charles would one day rest beside her. The stone was a plain one and she brushed away a new growth of moss from around the inscription. She would not break down.

There was no comparing loss with loss, but Charlotte's marriage had promised new life. D.O. was robbed of a daughter and a grandchild, and doubtless mourned again for his first wife and his partner Adamson. She would console him for these when she wrote back. It was the least she could do.

When she returned she was wet and tired. She spent the afternoon in her room, reading her Bible, before writing a brief note to her editor, rejecting his offer of a response.

Charles was already at the table when she went down to dinner. He rose to greet her and she saw he was wary of her mood. She kissed his cheek and apologised for her disproportionate reaction of the night before and said, 'I have thrown my response to Blenkinsop on the fire.'

His brow cleared at this return to more mundane matters. 'I think that's wise. McPherson will only publish her article if he has something from you.'

Her spirit was returning. 'And I will not give either of them the satisfaction.'

They enjoyed their soup in silence.

'You went to the grave, I hear.'

'Yes and I feel better for it. I've made my peace again.' She thought of the mossy stone. 'I do sometimes wish we had given her a name.'

He nodded in his thoughtful way. 'Your mother favoured Anne, I remember.'

'And you favoured Elizabeth. But I would have none of that.' The maid cleared away the soup dishes. 'We could have called her Charlotte, after you.'

He gave her a warning look. 'I think Anne would have been best.' He reached for her hand over the table and leaned towards her. Charles was not the kind to wink, but did she see a flicker in his eye?

'At any rate, never Jane.'

Dear Charles. He knew just how to cheer her up.

'No, never Jane,' she said.

They passed the evening reading passages to each other from favourite books.

The letter to Edinburgh could wait another day, but it would be done.

CHAPTER SEVENTEEN

His Glory Days

Amelia Hill, February 1863

After the funeral, D.O. retired into himself, hollow-eyed and broken hearted. If he came downstairs at all, he sat in the parlour, staring into the grate as he had on the day we buried his daughter with her newborn bairn. Our brief and joyful intimacy was broken. Then came the letters, battering at our door like January hail, just when we needed some peace.

My brother, his closest friend, called nearly every day, though D.O. would not see him. One morning in February Noel watched as I took another black-edged sheet from its envelope, running my eye over its elegant script.

'How is he doing?' Noel asked.

I shook my head. 'It's as if he hardly knows me. He sometimes asks if John Dalgleish has called. No one else is given a thought.' Chattie's husband had gone back to his own affairs, as folk must do after even the hardest of blows. My job was to keep others at an arms length. As well as the letter in my hand there were four more, all delivered that morning.

'He wants me to answer them. From folk I barely know.' We'd had so little time as man and wife. Now his past acquaintances came rushing at me as if a damn had been breached, the wave of cold water reminding me how little of his life I'd shared.

'I feel for you, Mamie, yet you can't blame him for being cast lower than he's ever been.'

'I cannot. But when he says he has nothing to live for, what can I say?'

'Tell him he has you, he has his friends.'

'Whom he says get on well enough without him.'

Noel shook his head. He nodded at the letter still in my hand. 'Who is it this time?'

'Lady Eastlake, if you will.' It was a kind letter, signed *Your loving friend, Elizabeth.*

Noel's face creased into a smile. 'I met her once in London, Elizabeth Rigby she was then, a towering girl with a sharp tongue. She and D.O. were very thick when she was in Edinburgh. When Adamson was alive,' he added.

Another icy wave engulfed me. All those years that meant so much to him and I had been no part of them. 'His glory days, he calls them.'

Noel took my hand. His pale eyes were all concern. 'Don't give up on him. He may have glories still to come.'

It was hard to imagine. In weeks his hair had gone from piebald brown to white. The flesh sagged on his cheekbones. My fine new husband was beginning to look like Old Father Time.

'Give me that letter,' Noel said. He nodded to himself as he read it. 'She spoke of him when I met her, you could see there was . . . affection there.'

There had been plenty of affection between D.O. and me when we were wed. Since the funeral he had turned away from me in our high bed. I was embarrassed to be offering a comfort he didn't want and so our hopes of another bairn, my bairn, were buried with Chattie.

When Noel left I was still holding the letter. The injustice of it all, the death so soon after our marriage filled me with frustration as well as grief. I needed to work, to bury my hot anger in a cold pile of clay. Except Noel was right. It was too soon to give up. We might have married late but D.O. and I were well-matched. I needed to put my pride to one side. He had been fond of Elizabeth. Maybe it was time to call on her for help.

In the bedroom he was sitting motionless in the bedside chair, looking at the wall, an unopened Bible beside him. I busied myself, tucking in the sheets and smoothing the quilt, making up for his stillness.

'Another letter has come,' I said. 'From one of yon girls, an old sweetheart, I dare say.'

His eyes took on some focus and he scowled from under his brows. 'Who then?'

I had got his interest, a small subterfuge was in order. 'I forget the name.'

'From Edinburgh?'

'I didn't look.'

'You could bring it to me.'

The letter was of more interest to him than I was. I tried not to taste the bitterness on my tongue. 'Your heart is broken, David, not your legs. I won't fetch and carry for you. The letter is downstairs on the sideboard.'

He left the room, which I counted a small victory. I listened to his slow and heavy footfall on the stairs, gave him a few minutes alone with his Elizabeth, then followed him down. I found him leaning on a chair, the letter in his hands, tears furrowing his cheeks.

Tears were better than silence. I wiped them with my hand, taking the letter from him. 'Come away, now. Why would this Elizabeth gar ye greet? Noel says you had fine times, the two of you.'

'We did. Fine times indeed. And we wrote after she left, for a wee while, but not after Robert.'

He transferred his weight from the chair to my shoulder and I was glad to feel the pressure of his hand. 'She lost her bairn, you know. Somebody told me and still I didn't write, thinking we were nothing to each other.'

The tears were back. It was the most he had said to me in weeks. I reached up and put my arms around him. 'There is nothing like troubles of your own to make you mind those of your fellow men.' I didn't move, feeling him holding back more tears, waiting for him to come to himself.

At length he gave a great sigh and let go of my shoulders. 'Elizabeth Rigby! We must have those calotypes somewhere.' His frown showed an old determination and he headed out of the room.

My plan had gone awry. As if it wasn't enough to read letters from his old loves, I must look for the murky pictures he had made of them. It wasn't what I'd envisaged when I called up the ghost of Elizabeth.

He found what he was looking for in my studio, his old darkroom, in a wall-press filled with albums and single pictures stacked in piles. He made space for the heavy books on the table, brushing away the film of plaster dust with a click of his tongue. There was no chair in the place, but he sat down on an old three-legged stool, opening each set of pictures, knowing at once if it was right or wrong, until he gave a quick sigh of triumph. He had found the album he wanted.

I stood behind him as Elizabeth Rigby stared back at us from every page, posed artfully in a manufactured bower or caught in a moment of less formality, dressed in some theatrical costume or in her everyday clothes. Always with those staring eyes and hair wound around her ears. In one she wore a gown with a low-cut neckline and bare shoulders. On the facing page, David looked towards her, with laughter in his eyes.

I left him to it. I had achieved what I wanted, to have him think of something other than his daughter's death. My new bust of Noel's son, half finished, gazed sightlessly down from a plinth in the corner of the room.

Our next visitor from his past came in person. I happened to go to the door myself and didn't recognise Jessie Mann straight away. I had met her only once before, at the funeral, one of many women with grey faces. When she said her name I remembered how she had been part of his household long before me.

In the parlour, Jessie took off her gloves. 'I'm sorry for your loss.'

Her face was lined with sadness but she smiled when she saw me looking at the black fingers of her right hand. 'It's the silver chloride,' she said. 'It never leaves you, though D.O. never got his hands dirty.'

I had no answer. We were back to the glory days, though this time it rankled less. D.O. had brought the albums in from the studio to the back room and conversed with the faces in them most afternoons. The past lived along side us. I couldn't embrace it but I had begun to accept it. Jessie, of course, knew far more about it than I did. After Adamson's death she was the one who had tidied and stacked the calotypes, keeping them safe for when they would be needed, never guessing the sad event that would bring D.O. back to them.

I assumed she expected to see him rather than me and I explained he was at the Academy.

'They threatened to find somebody else to take his place. He was so affronted he asked for his coat and went straight there.' The fire in him burned low but had not gone out completely.

Jessie nodded. 'Work is the best thing for him.'

I thought I should offer her tea, though she had called unannounced. Then why should she make an appointment when she had practically lived here at one time? A silence fell as I sorted through my thoughts.

'And how are you?' she said. 'It must be hard for you.'

It might have been no more than politeness, but this woman with the brown eyes was the first to have asked. I had to cling to the arm of the chair for fear I would give in to unexpected tears. I found a half smile. 'I am managing.'

But I am lonely, I could have said. My brother and his wife have other preoccupations, my husband and I step cautiously around a gulf of silence.

'So much hope, she said, 'swept away from you, from all of us.'

My loneliness was partly of my own making. I had been shutting myself away in my discontent just as D. O was nursing his grief. Jessie was part of the fabric of his life. She had come with condolences but she shared our loss.

'Thank you for coming,' I said to her. 'You must have known Chattie very well.'

I told her the story of taking Chattie to the burn in Dunfermline. She said the bairn had been both a joy and a trial in a house full of visitors. I told her about the letter from Elizabeth and how it had helped him but not me.

She smiled at the mention of her name. 'Oh, she was a character.'

I could have asked how close they had been, D.O. and Elizabeth, since Jessie would have known but I held back. How had it been for her, watching and helping, seeing so many men and women come and go, wondering sometimes where things might lead? More than that, what did it matter to me if Elizabeth had been his lover, or that he took comfort in his memories. These days were long past.

'I only want to be a good wife,' I said. 'And I don't think I am making much of a job of it. Maybe you can help me, Jessie.'

When I took her through to the back room she frowned at the pictures of Chattie turned to the wall. 'He should take pleasure in these,' she said. And so I went round and turned them to face us, the bairn on her father's knee, the girl by a pond with other wee lassies, and the one I liked best, the wee girl captured dancing in front of a mirror.

I took down his precious albums from the bookcase and laid them on the table where we could go through them together.

'Tell me about them,' I said. 'Not how they were made but who is in them, how he knew them, if they are family, friends or folk he barely knew.'

She did as I asked and I did my best to memorize the names and faces, to make some common ground between us of what had been alien territory.

After a while Jessie looked at the albums still on the table said, 'There should be more. Where are all the ministers?'

They still lay on the shelves of the wall press, untouched, like the painting in his upstairs studio. 'We have them still,' I said. 'He will go back to them in time. He needs a new occupation now, not an old one.'

It was a while before D.O. came back. He stopped at the door in surprise, greeted Jessie and stood behind me to see what we were at. The page in front of me held a very fine calotype of Robert Adamson with his family. I had never met the man but I guessed his quiet nature from the picture.

'Jessie has been showing me your glory days,' I said. 'Now you can show me too.'

That night he wept in my arms.

'Why did God bring me such unhappiness? Ann, Robert, Chattie, what did I do to lose them all?'

It was a relief to have him close to me and I felt something yield that had been holding firm for his sake. I shed silent tears into the shoulder of his nightshirt.

'Don't think you are singled out for sadness,' I said, smoothing his cheek. 'It's no more than many a body has to bear.'

He shifted onto his back, his arm still around my shoulders. 'I have been a selfish man, Mamie,' he said. 'And I am lucky to have you by my side.'

From then on he went back to his studio and I was free to go back to mine. We worked through our sadness doing the things we knew best. I can't say we were happy but what I had said to Jessie became true: we were managing.

CHAPTER EIGHTEEN

The Good Wife

Amelia Hill, June 1863

Our peace was temporary and came to an end on the day, a few months later, when I was called to the parlour to find three ministers standing in the window, blocking out the light. When I invited them to sit, they took the best chairs, folding their black wings around them. Of the three I knew only Doctor Candlish who had married us. From their demeanour, I sensed the others were senior to him but they let him take the lead. The cause of their visit wasn't hard to guess.

'We hate to trouble you at a difficult time,' Candlish said.

They would trouble me all the same, though rather me than my husband who as usual was out for the morning.

'You must see, Mrs Hill, how we need to have the matter resolved.'

Why beat about the bush? 'You mean you want the picture finished.'

The new Free Kirk Assembly Rooms were nearly built and glowered at me every time I passed below the Mound. The painting of the Disruption, which was to hang in them as a memorial to its founders, was a long way from finished and untouched since Chattie's death.

'It's too soon.' I said. 'He's in mourning.'

Some part of him would always be in mourning. I only hoped one day he would lock his grief away and walk straight again.

The men in front of me inclined their heads in polite condolence, like a row of wooden puppets. They showed no sign of giving way.

'We hear he is back at his desk,' one of them offered. 'And work is a great consolation.'

Labor omnia vincit. I couldn't argue with that. He and I were both finding solace in our different ways but the Disruption Painting had always been a burden. He would find no comfort there.

One of the ministers whose name had slipped past me beetled his brows. 'Of course this is also your husband's Holy Duty. As his wife you will not want him to fail in it.'

I wondered if they saw the flicker of annoyance in my face. D.O. was not a man to fail in any duty. A wife had duties too: to protect her man from his debtors and his grief.

I addressed Candlish whom I hoped would be the most merciful. 'I can't tell you the day or the month,' I said. 'But he won't fail you. You have my word.'

The interview was at an end. I stood up and they stood up with me.

If D.O. had promised the Kirk too much, I had put myself under the same obligation. I already felt my shoulders ache under the weight of the yoke.

Some instinct took me to Jessie Mann's house in Leopold Place. She had never called since the day we looked through the old calotypes but I needed somebody to confide in. I think I was hoping she would take my new burden away, although I should have known she wasn't a woman to argue with the Kirk.

If she was surprised to see me at her door she didn't show it and invited me into her modest but comfortable front room.

I took off my shawl. 'They were like the corbies that sit on our roof,' I said, 'cawing for food.'

'They're only asking for their due,' she said. 'What does D.O. have to say about it?'

I confessed I hadn't told him about the ministers. As soon as I said so, I saw how I was deceiving myself if I thought I could keep it from him. Jessie's look said the same.

'He might not talk about it,' she said, 'but do you think it's not on his mind? Do you think it hasn't been for twenty years?' Her eyes softened at my plight and his.

'The only way you can help him is to see it gets finished.'

Jessie and I would never share idle gossip or go looking for new hats on Princes Street. We would never be friends of that kind, but I had come to the right person.

'I promised them it would be,' I said. 'I just don't know how it's to be done.'

'The Disruption was the start of it all,' she said. 'Now he must make an end of it.'

For me the painting was a relic I would rather see buried. For Jessie we had simply come full circle. There was no doubt in her voice but it was tinged with regret. She had been part of this task too. As long as it continued, there would be a bond between her D.O. I could see a reluctance to let it go.

I thought of my husband who painted while turning his back to the canvas that took up most of the room. 'He is working on something new and he's taking pleasure in it. I don't want to see him cast down all over again.'

With Jessie, duty would always come first. She ignored my plea. 'How much is still to be done?' she asked.

I had studied it that morning. The leaders of the Disruption were complete. The rest was a mishmash of faces, some drawn only in outline with arms and legs dangling beneath, other faces painted in but with bodies missing.

I shook my head. 'It will still be many months, even if he were to spend every day on it.'

201

She nodded. 'It was always too big a task for one man. That's why he needed Robert.'

From the way she spoke his name I caught her deep affection for the man I had never known.

I thanked Jessie for her advice. I hadn't expected her to offer me a solution. If anything, I had hoped only for more time. She was right to tell me time was the last thing I had.

Her blackened fingers caught my eye and I thought back to all the albums we had studied and all the faces in them. 'Jessie, were there never any calotypes of you?'

Another quiet smile. 'Och I was always busy,' she said, 'developing and printing. And then there was the cost.' She narrowed her eyes. She was casting her mind back to all those days and months. 'Once or twice I posed for them to judge the distance or the light, but never with a paper in the slide. Anyway,' she gave a quick laugh. 'I won't be missed, an ordinary body who just wanted to help. And it was the same with Robert. How many pictures have you seen of him?'

D.O. flirted with the lens, Robert stood behind it. But not always. I would know Adamson's face if I came upon it. Only Jessie was missing from the record of those days. Or were there others who had never sat in front of the camera, others again whose pictures had been lost?

I left Jessie and walked up the hill, past the Observatory, over to where Edinburgh was laid out before me. Where once he had painted the city in a great sweep from the castle to the Forth, D.O.'s new canvas looked this way, from the Calton to St Giles, and it was small. He was pouring all his energy into a diminishing space. As I turned back down the hill I worried how I could draw him away from the occupation that brought him comfort, if not joy, and back to discharging his duty.

He had made his offer to the Kirk in the heat of the Disruption, in the prime of his life. In the chilly light of old age it was too heavy a burden. If only he had finished it at the time. Or had it always been beyond him? What Jessie said stuck in my mind no matter how the breeze tried to whip it away. The Disruption painting was too big for one man.

That night we dined as usual with his sister, Mary, and her husband, John. D.O. talked of what was happening in the galleries and some new commission that might go to Noel. I glimpsed a hint of happiness in him, or the prospect of happiness. I couldn't bring myself to cast him back into gloom.

There was only one road left to me. In the early morning I left him sleeping and stood in front of the painting that would cast a shadow over my marriage until it was done.

I had rarely worked in oils and the brush was awkward in my hand. I would rather have used my fingers to daub the canvas. But I persevered, beginning in the darkest of corners, touching black paint onto a boot, a trouser leg. When I had some feel for what I was doing, I changed my brush and loaded it with white to tackle the shirt fronts. I began to enjoy it, if only there had been less to do.

Behind me as I worked was the new painting, tiny by comparison, jewel-like in its intensity. When I finished up that day, still before our breakfast, I was drawn to it. The towers of Edinburgh glimmered silver and gold in the distance. The foreground was all darkness: the cemetery, dark shrubbery, a touch of light in the stone wall marking the boundary of Rock House. This painting would have something of himself in it. Since I had last looked he had added new details: a bairn's toys lay abandoned on the wall, on the grassy slope, shaded by bushes, I saw a figure sleeping and next to him a camera. The area was so dark I almost missed it, as if the artist wanted this to be private, seen only by those who looked closely into his soul.

So we went on, together and apart. In the afternoons I went to my studio and lost myself in the textures of wax and plaster and clay. He continued with his new view of Edinburgh, the vale of tears, as I called it to myself. Each day when I daubed at the ministers, its sad brilliance mocked my efforts.

One day there was a movement behind me. The brush was in my hand.

'Don't think I haven't seen what you're doing,' he said.

He put his hand on my shoulder and I laid down the palette. 'I'm sorry. I only started because the Kirk has been asking.'

His sigh said he had known all along. 'Don't be sorry. You're a good wife to me. Carry on with what you're doing. Many hands make light work.'

Just standing in front of the painting had made his shoulders slump. 'You'll maybe do better than me. Say what you think,' he pointed to the front row of ministers. 'They look like a row of tumshies.'

I wanted to laugh and tell him they were no such thing but his ministers, it had to be said, were all round in the face and of a similar mien. It must be hard to paint folk you hardly know however good a photograph you've made.

'Well the others,' I said, 'will just have to be tatties and beetroot.'

My joke fell flat which was no more than it deserved. I touched his arm. 'I know you want to finish it. That you care about the Kirk.'

I thought of the new painting behind us with all its warmth, its light and shade. It was hard to think it came from the same hand. I turned him to look at it.

'This is what you can do when you want to.'

He shrugged his shoulders. 'This is different.'

'Why is it? Tell me about it.'

'What is there to tell? I'm calling it *In Memoriam*.'

He had said as much at the dinner table two nights ago. 'In memory of Adamson and Chattie?'

He didn't correct me.

'It's very fine,' I said. 'The sadness gives it beauty, the beauty

204

gives you comfort. How do you think folk will see it in time to come? Will it be your greatest work?'

He looked puzzled. Folk would see a new view of Edinburgh. The meaning was important only to him.

In the corner of the room I had stacked all the calotypes of the ministers I could find. I picked up half a dozen and brought them to him, asking myself what Jessie would say. 'They deserve to be remembered too, for their faith, for their actions. They have husbands and wives, daughters, sons, parishioners who'd like to see them properly remembered.'

He leaned closer to me, his arm around my shoulder. 'I can see you're trying to make it easier for me. I haven't the heart for it but I know there is no escape. You must keep me to my word.'

He was looking at the figures I had worked on, seeing if they measured up. He was ready to carry on.

'I've given my word too. We can do it together.'

This was enough to lay on him that day. *In Memoriam* slid out of view as he renewed his acquaintance with the ministers. I wasn't sure his duty was enough to carry him to the end.

In my studio, the old wax birds from my father's house looked down on me from a high shelf. If I modeled a bird now it would be a different creature from the one I made when I was twenty. As many years had passed for D.O. since he began the painting. If he was a different man, maybe it could be a different painting, the one he needed it to be.

CHAPTER NINETEEN

Extraordinary Things

Jessie Mann, 1865

Amelia Hill invited me often enough to Rock House but the more I hesitated, the less inclined I was to go and somehow two years have come and gone. It's not that I'm jealous of the new wife. I watch them out and about in his old haunts and see that she's good for him. The stick he uses for walking has become a habit, more for effect than for support – a mark of seniority. He holds his head high and when he stops on a quiet corner to rub his eyes, only a friend would wonder if it's more then the wind making them smart.

I hear his great painting is nearly finished, another reason for us all to rejoice, though reminding his wife of her husband's duty on that score was maybe not the best start to a friendship. In any case, we would have made an unlikely pair, Amelia Hill with her artistic family and me, Jessie Mann, a woman from Perth who just likes to know how the world works.

Of course there are other reasons I walk past the house without turning up the steps or in at the garden gate and they have nothing to do with her. With every death, something is lost, not just from the future but from the past. I would like to leave my memories where they are, to let them crystallise in my mind where I can take then out and give them a polish when I feel the need. Rock House will see more life and death, more happiness and grief in time to come. If I go there I'll think only of those who will never come back.

I have to put these thoughts aside when D.O. calls. It gives me quite a turn to find him standing at my door. The last time was when he came back from St Andrews, from the other funeral. He is a different man now and I will never be used to all the white hair. Still, I catch some of the old light in his eye.

'I was just passing,' he begins. 'And thought we hadn't seen you for a while.'

Two years is more than a wee while but time passes us at different speeds. With the Kirk standing over him, his years have likely been quicker than mine. I ask him in and he stands in the living room, telling May he will keep his coat on as he isn't stopping. His voice is deeper than I remember.

'Have you heard, we're nearly there? The Kirk has had its pound of flesh.' He's making light of it, the thing that nearly had him on his knees. 'I have a good wife, you know, and I have you to thank for the help she has given me.'

I assume he's speaking in some general way. 'I've tried to be a good friend.'

There's a pause in which I look back over the times he and I have shared, the good and the not so good, in Perth, in Rock House, even on my misbegotten trip to Ayrshire. His smile lets me think he holds some of the same memories dear.

'You made her keep her promise and she's helped me keep mine. Mind you, she still struggles with using oils. She'll be pleased when she can give all her time to her sculpting, and so will I.'

It takes me a minute to catch his drift. 'She's doing your painting for you?'

He laughs. 'With me, Jessie, with me. There are still some things I can teach her. But she has made all the difference.' He leans towards me and gives me a nudge. 'I've told her that Hills will overcome mountains.'

Only D.O. could make such a terrible joke and expect me to laugh. I shake my head, smiling to myself at the upturn in his spirits.

'But I can't stand here all day. She would like you to come up. Tomorrow if you can. I know you won't let us down.'

He claps his hat on his head and heads for the door. I have no idea what's required of me but I'll have to go and find out.

I'm shown out the back, to Robert's old dark room. I hesitate on the threshold, preparing for shadows, but once inside I barely recognise it. The windows are uncovered and the place has a new clean smell. On the shelves where we kept the developer and fixing agents she has ranged models of small birds and animals. In between there are rough pieces of rock, quartz or granite, veined with pink or green. I would like to take a closer look but don't like to seem forward.

She is prodding at a head made of clay. 'My nephew, Diarmid,' she says. 'It has dried badly. I might have to start again.'

She has a vigour I haven't seen before. This is her world and her medium. When I told her to help her husband I took her away from it.

'You've given up your work for his.'

She looks up from her model. 'There was nothing else for it. I still come down here when I can find hours in the day.'

She gives her clay a final pummeling, and comes over to embrace me, keeping her hands away from my frock as I try to conceal my surprise at this unexpected closeness. Her hair is sleek and has a spicy scent. I remember she is only forty, as Robert would have been, had he lived.

She laughs off her clumsiness. 'I'm glad you came. I was beginning to think I had offended you.'

My eyes are still exploring the rest of the room. The walls

have been painted white. This is what has changed it so much. She stands back from me. 'Oh, I'm not thinking. This was your place before it was mine. I hope it doesn't upset you.'

I shake my head. 'It's good to see it put to a new use.'

She moves to the sink and washes her hands. There is a natural grace in her as there is in D.O. Does it come with being an artist, or simply knowing your place in the world?

'Come and see the painting. You must tell me what you think before the Kirk gives its verdict.'

I've seen it many times over the years and it never fails to astound me, the gallery of faces, row upon row. The finished article is even harder to take in and here in his studio we're too close to it. Wherever I look, four hundred pairs of eyes stare back at me. I have no words, I have no opinion to give, only a feeling of awe.

I dare say I'm not the first to be struck dumb. Amelia accepts my silent contemplation and takes up a brush and palette. Every minute is to be put to good use. Before she lays anything on the canvas, she glowers at the fine-haired implement in her hand as if its intention is evil. How alien it must be for her to use paints and brushes, as if I were to make a start with glass and collodion, or coat paper with the white of an egg for an albumen print.

'I'll never get used to it. David has done his best to show me. Noel too. This must be the first painting by a whole family.'

Her calling him David startles me, then I'm glad to hear it. His younger days have caught up with him.

The most striking part of the picture is Chalmers, in a ray of light like some Old Testament prophet, the Kirk's Messiah. I look for what's still to be done. There are precious few gaps in the crowd.

Amelia has put down her brush and points at the top of the painting, to the skylights of Tanfield Hall. I see how figures are leaning in at the high windows, one with a lum hat. Amelia sees my puzzlement. 'The Newhaven Folk,' she says.

I know all kinds were there that day. I picture the fishermen clambering up on the roof. My curiosity is engaged and I study the rest of the crowd. 'Not just the ministers, then.'

'No. Not just the ministers. Everybody who was there, or might have been.'

She watches me scanning the painting with new eyes, seeing how he has arranged them all, not just the churchmen but the other supporters of the Disruption, the Edinburgh public, exotic figures from abroad.

'So he has put in it whoever he likes?'

She shrugs.

'What will the Kirk have to say about that?'

She has gone back to painting in the details of a carved chair. Her brushwork must be better than she makes out. 'It's been twenty years in the making. It doesn't just belong to the Kirk any more. It belongs to the folk who were there, the folk who wanted the Disruption. It belongs to the man who has painted it.'

Her voice is untroubled but I sense a challenge. This is why she wanted me to come. I'm her sounding board. I'm standing in for the Kirk. I think of the day she called at the house and how I made no concessions. I consider where my loyalties lie, to the Kirk, surely, to the ministers who made their stand. I should state my case, tell her it will have to be changed.

As I fumble with my words I see D.O. is in the painting, sketchbook in hand, returned to his youthful glory. I have to smile. This is as it should be. He often talked about how he was there, though maybe not quite like this. Behind him a face makes me catch my breath. Robert, looking down into his camera; there's no mistaking the straight nose, the serious look, the long fingers. I can't hold back a cry. 'He has him to the life.'

'Adamson has as much right to be there as anybody. I'm only sorry I never met him.'

Robert was never at Tanfield. That day he was moving in

210

to Rock House, setting himself up in business, not standing behind D.O. in a roomful of ministers. They look right together, though, as they always did: D.O. with his artist's eye, Robert at his shoulder with his scientist's mind. Amelia Hill is right. It would be wrong to have one without the other. It satisfies me and it should satisfy the Kirk.

I run my eye over the canvas with a renewed interest. 'Who else is here that I know?'

Amelia nods to a group of women on the other side of the canvas. 'Did you ever know Ann?'

I did not. I met her sister once, a sweet natured woman who loved Chattie dearly. She will be pleased to have her sister remembered in this modest way, on the edge of the picture, subdued in tone. Ann and Robert amongst so many strangers.

'This is how you spurred him on.'

She smiles without looking up from her work. 'I told him this would be their memorial and his. What do you think? Will it pass muster with the Moderator?'

I watch the new Mrs Hill, adding some paint and scraping if it off again, a wife who saw how this picture could embody his love – for God and the Kirk, for his own kith and kin.

'I think you're right. It's his painting. He may honour anybody he likes.'

I'm intent on seeing how many faces I recognise but come back to Robert's. 'This is as fine as any calotype.'

There is a twinkle in her eye. 'Not all art needs the camera, Jessie, which is just as well. I have never taken a photograph in my life and don't intend to.'

She works on. Through the attic window, I glimpse a grey October afternoon with a blanket of cloud around the rooftops. There should be a ray of sun, like the beam of light in the picture, to settle around the shoulders of Amelia Hill, who has unlocked something so that she and her husband will be free of his old obligation.

'It can't have been easy for you.'

A short laugh. 'I don't know many folk whose lives have been easy,' she says. 'Noel, I suppose, has had the best run up to now, and, God willing, the blessing of his bairns.'

This is something else she has given up for him, although she has other ways of making life.

She lays down her brush and her eyes are on mine. 'And what about you Jessie? What things have you found hard?'

I'm startled she has been thinking of me, as I have been thinking of her, each of us keeping a respectful distance. Now that she has asked me to say my piece. I don't hesitate.

'My brother used to say *panta rhei*. Nothing, and no-one, lasts forever. That was even before my mother died. Chattie's death? I feel it more for D.O. than for myself.' I have to take a breath. 'In Perth I had two brothers I looked after as bairns. They never grew up. Robert was the nearest I came to having them back, or having a son of my own. And he had sic a way with him. His passing was the hardest to bear.'

She nods as if she has known all of this. 'You should be beside him then, or as close as we can get you. Come and sit down.'

This isn't the place to sit for a blether or a cup of tea. There's only one plain chair. She's smiling at my incomprehension. 'That man of mine never took your calotype and I'm not going to try. I'll make a sketch. Who knows it might be every bit as good.'

What would I want with a portrait at my age? If she wants to thank me there are other ways.

'Look,' she's pointing to the painting, to a row of women above and behind Robert. 'We've left a place for you.'

As she goes downstairs to find her sketching pad, I sink down on to the chair, imagining me, Jessie Mann, in the great Disruption Painting. When she comes back I tell her my head is birling with the idea a woman like me should stand amongst the gentry.

'Not just gentry, Jessie,' she says, and I remember the Newhaven fishermen at the window.

'And you've seen some wonders,' she says, 'as many as I have.'

She has traveled in Europe, visited London. I've been lucky to see wonders on my own doorstep. As I settle myself for the sitting, the sun puts out a gleam of reddish gold at last, not just in her honour but in mine, an ordinary woman who has seen extraordinary things.

I'm not deceived. I'll be one of many faces whose names will be forgotten. But I've played my part, stood behind the Disruption, helped with the impossible task of painting it. I've known two men whose names will be remembered.

Amelia sets to work. 'Keep looking away from me,' she says. 'You'll be in profile.'

There's a hush of charcoal on the paper. The sun touches my face. In my mind's eye, my chair is in the open air. The slide is in the camera. D.O. is standing to one side, weighing up the angle of the light. The lens cover comes off. Robert's fingernail taps a rhythm on the camera as he studies his watch.

He looks up. 'That's it!' he says. 'We're done!'

The cover is replaced. The eye closes.

WAYS AHEAD

CHAPTER TWENTY

In the Blink of an Eye

May 1866

Scobie's train was due to leave in an hour but Louisa's father lived near Greyfriars Kirk. He would have to hurry to get there and back to the station in time. Unless of course he changed his plans. Since leaving Tanfield, he had felt more at ease with himself so anything was possible.

When he reached Princes Street, he paused to watched the sun casting its tawny light over the city. Before him was the National Gallery, its strong and graceful lines a new embellishment to the place they already called the Athens of the North. Scobie would never visit Athens but if there had been time he would have gone inside this other Parthenon and acquainted himself with Gainsborough and other artists whose names he barely knew. He could have learned more about how painters addressed themselves to their work, with or without the aid of a camera. Maybe he still would, one of those days.

He was ready to cross the road and hurry up past the gallery when his eye settled on a figure emerging from the deep shadows on the eastern side of the building, an old man, leaning on a stick, supported on his other side by a woman in navy silk. The figures drew nearer and, as the sun caught them, it threw the man's profile into relief. Scobie looked again and shook his head in case he was mistaken. But he was not. This was Hill, the painter of the picture he had come to see. Scobie stopped in surprise, reflecting on the irony of almost bumping into him at the end of such a day, shocked at the change he saw in him.

In his mind, Hill had been a man forever in his prime. Scobie remembered him in his courtyard studio, flitting from camera to subject and back again, looking to his partner for confirmation of the pose and of where the shadows fell, his movements easy and lithe, his expression never anything but amiable. Even in the dwindling light, Scobie was struck by how much he had aged, a sight more than Walter Fairlie in the same time.

The couple turned east along Princes Street. The old man's progress was slow. Maybe he was heading for the Calton Rooms to admire his achievement and accept the adulation of the crowd. The remnants of Scobie's anger stirred. This could be his chance to confront the source of his disappointment, to ask Hill why some had earned a place in his painting and others had not, to tell him how far he had brought him on a fool's errand.

Scobie followed them, pondering the words he would use to make his accusation. In front of the Scott Monument, the woman, surely his wife, patted the artist's arm and left him as she went to inspect the statues around its base. Hill hirpled over to a seat provided for passers by. Scobie drew closer and, as he went forward, the old man raised his eyes to him as if expecting a greeting or a question, accustomed, it seemed, to being accosted by strangers in the street.

Scobie nodded to him. It was a proud face but there was a darkness in it, the eyes on the crowded scene but also elsewhere, on something or someone distant and deeply missed. The rounding of his shoulders spoke of sorrow more profound than anything resulting from Scobie's travails with awkward deacons or choirs who couldn't hold a tune. The once full cheeks were sunken. In the years he had given to his work, what had D.O. Hill lost along the way?

Scobie had meant to speak but he hesitated. There was a voice in his ear he could have sworn was Fairlie's, *Is this what you came for?* Scobie turned but it was only a stranger hurrying past.

The question still needed an answer. He had come to give thanks to God for the spirit that had made the new Kirk. Hill had given his thanks in the only way he knew. He had put his talents at God's disposal and filled his painting with those who had done the same, be they writers or scientists, fishermen or ministers' wives. Scobie met Hill's eye. Who was he to break an old man's reverie with petty complaints? He had not come to berate an artist over a painting. The man deserved some peace.

Hill was still waiting for him to speak.

'What a fine day to see the city,' Scobie said, as if they were both visitors out for the day, then turned away without waiting for a reply.

To get to Greyfriars, Scobie could turn back and up the Mound or continue along to the Waverley Bridge. He was still in the shadow of the Scott Monument and let his eyes ascend to where its apex pierced the sky. The words of the psalmist came back to him.

Come, and the works that God hath wrought.

Surely God had had a hand in the building of this spire, as well as in the cathedrals and kirks of the city. Godliness, he was beginning to see, took many forms and could be discerned in the hand of the stonemason and the sculptor, perhaps in the pen of the writer himself as long as his purpose was to glorify The Almighty. And if a writer or sculptor, why not the painter of four hundred ministers, pledging themselves to their Kirk?

The Calton Rooms were just beyond Waverly Station. In Scobie's memory, the Disruption Painting shone under the lantern roof in new resplendence, showing the adoration of the people not for Chalmers or for Hill, but for the God they both worshipped. He could go and take another look, scour the rows of faces again to find his own, but there was no need. If one man had been missed, God was still glorified. He would thank His own as He saw fit.

As for the walk to Tanfield Hall, Scobie was pleased the place had been locked up. What would have been the point in standing alone in its godless emptiness? The Painting showed it in the way it should be remembered. Nor would any future son of the Free Kirk have to walk up Dundas Street and over the Water of Leith now that the artist had thrown open the doors of the old gasworks hall and immortalised the greatest event to have taken place under its roof. Tanfield could be razed to the ground and replaced by something else. The Disruption Painting would live on. The painter had done what was asked of him.

To get to Blairgowrie required two trains. On the first, Scobie watched the country rolling past. At this time of year, the darkness was more a softening of the light. On the next train he dovered, grateful to the deacons for paying for his second class seat, watching the faces he'd encountered on his journey reflected in the murky carriage windows: the uncle he had dined with in Granton, Walter Fairlie, Mr Hill, the faces in the painting, None of them – the realisation made him smile – belonged to Louisa. He had thought better of going to her father's house, of asking her, a woman in her middle years, to leave the life she had chosen. His letter, guarded so carefully, would go on the back of the fire but it had served its purpose, steering him south on a journey he was glad to have made.

He considered its outcome in a new honesty of spirit. The visit to Auld Reekie had been no act of celebration. The gall of his anger, nursed for so long, had been too bitter to be assuaged by a day in the city and a look at a painting. But his erring soul had been right in its instinct to go and he had become, for the course of an afternoon, a humble pilgrim. His omission from the painting, though troublesome, no longer rankled. He had forgiven the artist who had a greater purpose than the inclusion of one newly-ordained minister. In forgiving D.O. Hill, he forgave himself his pride and the paucity of his faith.

That Sunday Scobie preached a sermon taking as his text Psalm 66, the fifth verse. The work of men, builders, artists, writers, should be praised, he told them, as long as its purpose is the Glory of God.

Jock Crawford, the session clerk, applauded the sermon and said would he take a high tea with them the following week? Mrs Crawford and Elspeth were both keen to hear about the wonders of Edinburgh.

And so Scobie found himself in Jock's best room, replete with Mrs Crawford's mutton pie and fruit cake. The Disruption Painting, he told them, was a masterpiece.

'If the deacons can buy a copy to hang in the Session House, it will be a token of our faith.'

Crawford sucked his teeth and said the deacons might be hard pressed to find the funds, but that was the way with deacons. He would see what he could do.

Jock, Scobie thought, would be as good as his word. He pictured the elders studying the rows of faces and smiled to himself at how long they might spend in a fruitless search for his own. At least Walter Fairlie had gained his rightful place amongst the ministers.

'Tell me, Jock,' Scobie said. 'Did you not have family Gilmerton way?'

Jock said he did and corresponded regularly with a cousin on his father's side.

Scobie recounted his meeting with Fairlie. 'I might write to him. He left all of a sudden and I'd like to thank him for his company.' And for his advice, he could have added, though he still wasn't sure how much had come from Fairlie and how much from his own conscience.

Crawford's forehead creased. 'Now it's funny you should say that.' He got up from his seat. 'Just haud on and I'll get the letter. It only came the other day.'

As he got up to burrow in the bureau, Elspeth smiled. 'You look better for your trip, Mr Scobie.'

He thanked her and said he felt better for it too.

Jock came back with a sheet of paper in his hand, hesitating before he spoke. 'Dear me, I thought as much. I'm sorry to tell you, your Mr Fairlie is gone.'

Outside, the wind stirred the laurel bush, causing a branch to clatter against the window and the sun to keek out from behind a scudding cloud. For a second, until the sun retreated, Scobie could have sworn he saw Fairlie with his grizzled hair and flinty eyes standing on Agnes Crawford's carpet, smiling his wrinkled smile.

Jock was reading from the letter. 'Tam says he came back from the Assembly with a chill and took to his bed. He's to be buried next week.'

Agnes drew her shawl around her, feeling the chill of bad news. Elspeth leaned forward in her seat with a look of concern. 'Did you know him well?'

Scobie saw the sharp eyes and heard Fairlie's words in his ear. 'We only met once, so no. Not as well as he seemed to know me.'

Agnes Crawford asked if Fairlie had been a good age. Scobie said yes, and they agreed it was likely his time had simply come.

Jock asked if he would go to Fairlie's funeral and Scobie said he would not. It was too far and he had other things to do. 'Let me talk to the deacons about the painting, Jock. Fairlie is in it too, you know. And rightly so.'

There was nothing like death to break up a gathering. Scobie said it was time he should go. Elspeth was close behind him as he was shown to the door. 'Blairgowrie will seem very quiet after Edinburgh,' she said, her voice still soft with concern.

'I don't think so,' Scobie replied. 'It's fine to be away but I have plenty to keep me here.'

He walked back to the manse in the stiffening breeze and went to his study. He would write a letter to the widow telling her how her husband would be remembered in the new Assembly Rooms. The sun was still coming and going as he took up his pen. Was it a trick of the light that had brought Walter Fairlie to the Crawfords' parlour and to his side on an Edinburgh afternoon?

God worked in mysterious ways, nobody could deny, like the dark slide taken from a camera and coaxed into life. Scobie reached for his Bible and Corinthians 13:12 *For now we see through a glass, darkly.*

He had another sermon to write and he knew where he would begin.

Notes on Chapters

Numerous Hill and Adamson images can be found online using a search engine. The images which inspired individual chapters are listed below with collection reference numbers. You can use these to identify each picture exactly. There are a few additional notes on other sources. A short list of books and articles follows.

Key to collections:
NGS National Galleries of Scotland: www.nationalgalleries.org
STAU St Andrews University Special Collections: www. st-andrews.ac.uk/library/specialcollections
GUL Glasgow University Library: www.gla.ac.uk/myglasgow/ specialcollections/collectionsa-z/hilladamson

2. Harebells in Barley
Images: *David Brewster* (STAU: ALB-24-71), *St Andrews Cathedral* (STAU: ALB-6-36), *Spindle Rock* (STAU: ALB-23-17), *St Andrews Harbour* (STAU: ALB-77-1)
Sources: I found documentary evidence of Jane Adamson although she appears in no family images.

3. The Restless City
Images: *Rev Thomas Chalmers* (STAU: ALB-77-7, NGS: PGP HA 552)
Many other images of ministers and groups of ministers can be found e.g. *Dumbarton Presbytery* (STAU: ALB-24-35)
Sources: Most information on Jessie Mann is to be found in Roddy Simspon's article of 2002. (See list of articles, p.230)

4. *The Bird of Wax*
Images: *D.O. Hill and Charlotte* (STAU: ALB-24-28)
Dunfermline Abbey, an engraving from a D.O. Hill original,
is of a later date.

5. *The Charm of the Man*
Images: *Miss Elizabeth Rigby* (STAU: ALB-24-19), *Mrs Rigby*
(STAU: ALB-24-17)

6. *The Absence of George*
Images: *George Meikle Kemp, Architect of the Sir Walter Scott
Monument* (NGS: PGP EPS 147)
Sources: Bonnar, T., *Biographical sketch of George Meikle
Kemp: architect of the Scott Monument, Edinburgh*. William
Blackwood, 1892 or via Internet Archive https://archive.org/
details/biographicalske00bonngoog

7. *The Morning After*
Images: *Edinburgh Ale* (NGS: PGP HA 435), *The Morning
After* (NGS: PGP HA 2254)

8. *Silver Harvest*
Images: *Mrs Elizabeth (Johnstone) Hall*, (NGS: PGP HA 301)

9. *Pas de Deux*
Images: *Lady Elizabeth (Rigby) Eastlake* (NGS: PGP HA 2258)
Sources: Elizabeth Rigby's article on Modern German Painting
appeared in the Quarterly Review, Vol 77, March 1846

10. *In the Shadow of the Door*
Images: *The Adamson Family* (GUL: HA0336)

12. *The Braes of Ballochmyle*
Images: *The Ballochmyle Viaduct* (GUL: HA0861)
Sources: for details of Monica Thorp's article of 1989 on Ballochmyle, see list of articles p.230.

13. *All His Darlings*
There are very few images of Charlotte (Chattie) Hill other than the one mentioned in *Bird of Wax* and the image used for the cover of this book. The whereabouts of the portrait bust by William Brodie is unknown.

15. *Open to Interpretation*
Mary Brodie was a sculptress and her husband was embroiled in a scandal over his first wife's death. Rockville was demolished in the 1960s. A photograph may be found on *The Scotsman* website.

16. *A Day of Ghosts*
Charlotte Dalgleish (nee Hill) died in childbirth in December 1862, a month after D.O. Hill married Amelia Paton.
Elizabeth Rigby/Eastlake's review of *Jane Eyre* can be read via the British Library website: www.bl.uk/collection-items/review-of-jane-eyre-by-elizabeth-rigby

The Disruption Painting

The painting, regarded as more of a curiosity than a masterpiece, resides in the Assembly Rooms of the Free Church of Scotland but is occasionally displayed in exhibitions elsewhere. I have seen it more than once and no reproduction or online image quite does it justice. However, there is a decent pull-out version in John Fowler's *Mr Hill's Big Painting* and a useful discussion of the later carbon print on the Photoseed Blog https://photoseed.com/blog/2014/08/23/permanence-of-disruption

Amelia Hill states in a letter (referred to in books by Sara Stevenson and Roddy Simpson) that she helped with its completion.

Selected Books, Articles, Web Resources

STEVENSON, SARA (2002)
The Personal Art of David Octavius Hill, Yale University Press, ISBN 978-0300095340

STEVENSON, SARA (2002)
Facing the Light: the Photography of Hill & Adamson, Scottish National Portrait Gallery ISBN 1-903278-32-5

RODGER, ROBIN H. (2002)
The Remarkable Mr Hill, Perth Museum and Art Gallery, ISBN 0-907495-20-6

FOWLER, JOHN (2006)
Mr Hill's Big Picture, Saint Andrew Press, ISBN 0-7152-0823-3

SHELDON, JULIE (2009)
The Letters of Elizabeth Rigby, Lady Eastlake, Liverpool University Press, ISBN 9781846311949 (Also available as pdf from www.oapen.org)

SIMPSON, RODDY (2012)
The Photography of Victorian Scotland, Edinburgh University Press, ISBN 978-0-7486-5460-4

ARTICLES
SIMPSON, RODDY
Amelia, the Artistic Mrs D.O. Hill, The Scots Magazine, June 2002, p.617-621

SIMPSON, RODDY
The Elusive Miss Mann, The Scots Magazine, July 2002, p.97-99

THORP, MONICA
Hill and Adamson without Adamson; the Ballochmyle Calotypes, Scottish Photography Bulletin, No 2, 1989, p.25-29

WEB RESOURCES
A detailed and practical account of making a calotype according to the methods of John and Robert Adamson is given by Rob Douglas, Twenty-First Century Calotypist: www.papershadowsandlight.com/dr-john-adamsons-process

Lightning Source UK Ltd.
Milton Keynes UK
UKHW02f2227150318
319529UK00006B/457/P